Only in Tokyo

Only in Tokyo

Two chefs, 24 hours, the ultimate food city

MICHAEL RYAN & LUKE BURGESS

Hardie Grant

BOOKS

Japan, and Tokyo in particular, has been my muse for decades. Every trip brings a little more depth to my understanding of this complex, multi-layered city. But it is enormous, and spatially it can be confusing, particularly when you travel mostly underground. A more manageable way of comprehending Tokyo is to think of it as a number of smaller cities merged into one — Shibuya, Shinjuku, Ikebukuro, Ginza … Each one has its own feel, its own personality.

The restaurant scene can be equally bewildering. With something like 160,000 restaurants in Tokyo, there is a problem of too much choice. Where do you start? I like to break it down into styles of food. When visiting, I always try to have sushi, ramen, yakitori and an izakaya meal at least once. But your preferences may lean in other directions. Make your own itinerary, but leave space for serendipitous discoveries. The thing with Tokyo is that on your walk to your lunch or dinner booking, you will without fail pass a number of other restaurants that look just as enticing as the one you are heading to.

Also think about the level of restaurant that you would like to dine at. Tokyo has some of the world's best high-end restaurants, as pointed out by the number of Michelin stars. But you can eat very well at all levels in Tokyo, from cheap ramen, to mid-range izakaya, to gastro temples. Mixing it up is the best approach.

Don't expect or attempt to get a handle on the entire city, even if you have a number of trips under your belt. Feeling like you will never truly know the place is partly what is so fascinating about it. And if you allow some flexibility in your plans, you will end up at some unexpected places that could well be the highlight of your trip. I guess I've been there just under twenty times now, and every visit is different — each one a bit of a 'choose your own adventure'.

As always, I can't wait to go back.

— Michael

This book can be credited to what is known as the 'Tokyo effect' – a gradual and considered exploration that supersedes the initial onslaught of lights, sounds and tremendous crowds. Two people, many stories: our foray into the societal fabric of Tokyo, the capital of one of the most fascinating cultures of the world.

So familiar yet so foreign. If Japan is enigmatic, then Tokyo is the heart of that riddle, its rhythm and essence so utterly alluring that it demands to be explored. It has a depth that keeps travellers in a constant state of rapture and delight. Whatever your vice, Tokyo has it covered.

Eating and travel photography happen to be my vices, and it's mission impossible to call it a wrap every time I leave Japan. More often than not, I'm contemplating the next encounter with leads from new discoveries and old friends. No one trip is the same, but familiarity grows a little each time.

I feel tranquillity in Tokyo, even though it is the largest populated metropolitan area in the world. The feeling seems counterintuitive, yet Tokyo begs you to relax and enjoy each layer, facet or slice of whatever you may have stumbled upon, or booked months in advance – always in the knowledge that you're without a hope of ticking all boxes, even in a lifetime of tours.

This book, a fine sliver, is just one narrative to begin your journey. Suggestions have been compiled from friends and colleagues who live and breathe Tokyo on a daily basis, and who call that behemoth of an industry – hospitality – their home. From here you have a starting point to create your own relationship with this captivating city, and to plot a course that can happen only in Tokyo.

– Luke

How to Use This Book

This book is a personal account of our favourite areas, restaurants and food haunts, and our attempt to share some of our knowledge and love of this city.

It is also a snapshot of the lives and work of some of the more creative people we know working in hospitality in Tokyo. These are friends we have built up over our many trips to Japan. With their knowledge and generosity – recommending the places they love to eat – each trip we make is even better than the last.

Most of the venues featured in this book are swayed toward the west of Tokyo, and in particular the wards of Shibuya, Shinjuku, Meguro and Minato. Most of our friends who have contributed live and/or work in these areas, and naturally their recommendations lean towards them. People in large cities tend to live and play in smaller village-like locales, and Tokyo is no exception. It is these enclaves that we seek out when travelling – we aim to live like locals, if only for a brief moment.

The venues have been loosely collated in the progression of a day, starting with breakfast and coffee stops, moving on to places to visit for lunch, then in the mid-afternoon, for dinner, and late at night … We stress 'loosely', as many of the venues are open through the day.

You will find all the classic foods of Japan, and more. Sushi, takoyaki, ramen, sandwiches, burgers done brilliantly, donuts. There are izakayas, tea houses for immersing yourself in the world of green tea, and high-end restaurants for witnessing the work of Tokyo's top chefs.

Use this book to give you a flavour of Tokyo, and to point you in some tasty directions. But know that it will not show you all of Tokyo. This is, in fact, not possible; the city is so big that no-one can ever truly 'know' it. Your fear of missing out needs to be discarded. Tokyo offers so many choices, so many permutations, that chance encounters and casual chats with restaurant staff lead to other new discoveries, which themselves lead to more. If we were to give one piece of advice when travelling to Tokyo, it is that you need to be flexible and have gaps in your itinerary for the unexpected. Following these threads will often lead to your fondest memories.

Our Team of Experts

Michael Ryan
Chef & Author

Luke Burgess
Chef & Photographer

Kan Morieda
Chef

Kullen Ozeki
Concierge

Masahira Onishi
Barista

Melinda Joe
Journalist

Hiroyasu Kawate
Chef

Robbie Swinnerton
Restaurant Critic

Zaiyu Hasegawa
Chef

Ayaka Makino
Sommelier

Makiko Iitsuka &
Kenichi Yamamoto
Sommelier & Chef

13

Camelback

Why
The best sandwich in Tokyo

What to ask for
Prosciutto, shiso and
yuzu baguette

Where
42-2 Kamiyamacho,
Shibuya-ku

When
8 am–5 pm
(closed Monday)

Camelback is an unlikely shop in a city full of unlikely shops.

Set up by Hayato Naruse, an ex–sushi chef, it's a sandwich shop done with the obsession for detail that the Japanese are renowned for. The country can certainly lay claim to some of the world's greatest sandwiches – the tonkatsu (crumbed pork) sando found throughout Japan and the ham and egg sandwiches from Lawson stores are prime examples, though they are of a particular style, with fluffy white bread being a main feature. To get a good crusty roll with fresh fillings is a little harder in Japan, but this hole-in-the-wall establishment just off the main thoroughfare of the increasingly cool and urbane Tomigaya/ Kamiyamacho area is one of your better choices.

They offer a small number of sandwiches, each carefully crafted and all very good. Their egg sandwich features tamagoyaki, or rolled omelette, which you may be familiar with from sushi restaurants. Their signature sandwich is a ham sandwich, but done through a prism of Japanese ingredients – shiso leaf and freshly grated yuzu rind alongside prosciutto. It almost sounds too simple to work, but the balance is perfect. Naruse-san cures his own lamb 'bacon' for another sandwich finished with coriander and dried tomato.

This being Japan, the sandwiches aren't foot-longs, and are all the better for it. They make a perfect mid-afternoon snack, or a light lunch when you know you have a multiple-course dinner ahead (which can be often in Tokyo).

The coffee, too, is good enough to come here just for that; it's on the darker side of the roast spectrum.

17

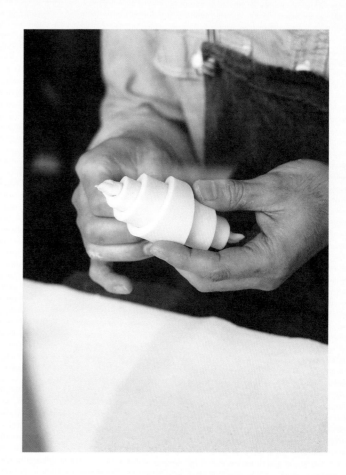

Path

___

Who recommended
Kullen Ozeki

Why
Fits all your needs,
be it breakfast, lunch or dinner

What to ask for
Dutch pancakes

Address
1-44-2 Tomigaya, Shibuya-ku

Hours
8 am–2 pm and 6–11 pm
(closed Monday and
occasionally Sunday)

Breakfast in Tokyo has always been tough.

The city is slow to wake, with many shops not open until 10 or 11 am. But things are changing a little, and some places are offering good breakfasts. World Breakfast Allday (3-1-23 Jingumae, Shibuya-ku) opens at 7.30 am and offers a monthly rotating breakfast plate from somewhere around the globe (think Lebanese one month, Finnish the next), as well as a standard menu offering a full English breakfast and porridge. As you'd expect from the name, they serve breakfast all day, until 8 pm. They are licensed as well, with drinks from around the world, so you can have a VB (Victoria Bitter – it's exotic here) with your toast if you want to.

Another great breakfast venue is Path in Tomigaya, Shibuya – in the up-and-coming area just west of Yoyogi Park. It has a casual neighbourhood vibe with sophistication and confidence. It is open during the day as a cafe, then again at night as a restaurant. With a minimalist design, record player, open kitchen and natural wines, it has all the prerequisites of a cool, modern restaurant. And it has the skills and creativity in the kitchen to match. Breakfast includes excellent coffee (pour-over) and a small but interesting selection of dishes, from quiche with gingko nuts, to their signature baked Dutch pancakes with prosciutto and burrata, to some of the finest croissants I have ever eaten – you can see these being made in-house at the front of the restaurant at certain times of the morning. The reason the food is so good here is partly because the chef, Taichi Hara, and the pastry chef, Yuichi Goto, worked at Cuisine[s] Michel Troisgros in Shinjuku, and the precision and attention to detail they learned is very apparent.

These skills are further showcased when Path reopens each day after a short afternoon break, offering what is possibly one of the best bargain set menus in Tokyo – seven courses of refined, creative cooking for under 6000 yen, and an optional wine pairing that is equally reasonable.

Path covers so many bases, from coffee stop, to breakfast, brunch and lunch venue, to wine bar, to restaurant. It is the sort of establishment you would love to have as your local.

Nem Coffee

Who recommended
Masahiro Onishi

Why
Quality coffee with
an international vibe

What to ask for
Coffee and a toasted sandwich

Where
4-5-6 Minami-Azabu, Minato-ku

When
8 am–5 pm
(closed Tuesday and first and
third Monday of the month)

Nem Coffee is as urbane and multicultural as its neighbouring suburb of Hiro-o.

The area is home to many of Tokyo's embassies and international schools, so the mix of nationalities is far greater here than in many other parts of Tokyo. It is an affluent area, with a serenity and quietness to it, and it can be surprisingly green in parts.

You might assume a cafe in this very residential sector could be tempted to play it safe, but in Tokyo you find great venues wherever you go. Nem Coffee is located down such a quaint little lane, you might also think you are headed in the wrong direction when looking for it, but remember, in Tokyo location is less important than the space itself (find the space, build your venue – they will come).

Nem Coffee resides in a two-storey building, tightly bookended by others, and stands out with its glass doors and windows and lush potted garden. Inside the plant theme continues with large plants in the corners, and a warm wooden service bar and tables. It is bigger than many cafes in Tokyo, but not by Western standards.

The wife-and-husband team have worked many years in the coffee industry, and it shows in the quality of their brews. Espresso, pour-over and press coffee are all offered. Food is simple but tasty – the toasted sandwiches are a good choice.

Even though the place has an international feel in its influences and clientele, Nem Coffee remains distinctly Japanese. Coffee houses here have a different approach to the busy, sometimes hectic cafes you might be familiar with. Take your time, be patient, speak a little quieter than you normally would. Relax.

Kullen Ozeki

The art of the concierge obviously requires an extensive knowledge of a city – the food, people, culture, fashion, style, architecture, night-life. You also need a network of connections, and maybe a touch of the psychologist, sometimes even the clairvoyant.

I first met Kullen when he was chief concierge at the Aman. This is one of Tokyo's most high-end hotels, with the demanding clientele to match. You would imagine that being chief concierge could be quite a stressful job, but Kullen was always cool, calm and collected. Serene almost. This partly comes from his seriously deep knowledge of Tokyo. I would say Kullen knows Tokyo just about as well as anyone could.

Kullen was born to Japanese-American parents and lived in Los Angeles until the age of twelve, when his family moved to Tokyo. There was some movement back and forth between Tokyo and LA, until the move became permanent during high school. Kullen says that the transition from American to Japanese schools and culture was challenging and pretty rough, but Tokyo is now his home with no plans to ever leave.

He started at the bottom in his hotel career, doing all and any jobs that came up – pool maintenance, bellhop, car-park attendant, cook, dishwasher, working the front desk. An opening in a concierge team arose, and Kullen knew this was where he wanted to be.

Kullen feels that his time at the Aman was the culmination of the first chapter of his life as a concierge. The next chapter involved the creation of his own service, Conciergest – a private and personalised agency for those who want to see a deeper side of Tokyo.

Artless Coffee

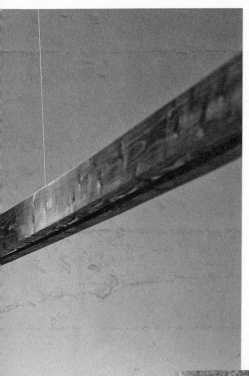

Who recommended
Kullen Ozeki

Why
Serenity with your coffee

What to ask for
Fine pour-over coffee
(they also do excellent green tea)

Where
2-45-12 Kamimeguro, Meguro-ku

When
11 am—8 pm daily

Tokyo is the home of the idiosyncratic coffee house.

Sure, the scene is dominated by the big players – Starbucks, Doutor, Tully's, Excelsior – but there are now so many interesting and unique coffee shops in Tokyo that you don't have to go to those, unless you're really desperate for caffeine or wi-fi.

Artless Coffee is certainly one of the more stylish independent coffee houses. It's so minimalist in design and effortlessly cool (anything but artless), I can't help but feel a little shabby when I walk into this place. And there is a good explanation for it: the shop is an extension, physically and conceptually, of the art gallery next door run by artist and interior designer Shun Kawakami. Around the shop are a number of Kawakami's stunning works featuring gold and silver leaf and handmade paper. While the art gallery is by-appointment only, the coffee shop is open to all.

There is precision and meticulousness at every level, from the items displayed for sale, to the cups you drink from, to the practised, serene way the coffee is made. The coffee here is pour-over, and the beans are sourced from three different roasters and changed seasonally.

You don't come here for a quick coffee slam-down – pour-overs take time. This place is not the busy, loud, social cafe that many in Western countries would be used to. If anything, its ambience is more aligned with a Japanese tea ceremony. Come here and take your time, and savour the wait.

Taking a liking to our server's jacket, I enquired as to where he bought it. He replied, 'It's a one-off and it's priceless.' The ultimate staff uniform.

UNU Farmers' Market

The Tokyo farmers' market scene is not on the level of other major cities, perhaps because Japan never succumbed to mega supermarkets.

Supermarkets in Japan are generally smaller, more personal affairs with high-quality meats, fruits and vegetables.

But the farmers' markets that do exist in Tokyo are great, and the one in front of the United Nations University is the best known. As with all great farmers' markets, the place has an air of celebration about it. If you're lucky, you might see some of Tokyo's chefs shopping here. There are usually fifty or so vendors, with a good range of fruits, some amazing varieties of daikon, fresh lettuces and other greens. The market is also the place for small-batch producers of honey, coffee, tea, jams, cakes and muffins. There is even a stall that produces some wonderfully scented sesame oil on-site. You can't help but wish there was a little less plastic, but this is Japan, the home of over-packaging.

If all the produce starts making you hungry, there are also plenty of food vans. The tiny roast meat van is one of the best – literally crammed with various roasted and smoked meats, to the point that it takes you a while to realise there's also a chef inside. Other great vans are the Japanese omelette van and Japanese curry van. There are coffee and beer vans, too.

Why
See just how important food
is to the people of Tokyo

What to ask for
Samples – lots of stalls are happy
for you to try before you buy

Where
5-53-70 Jingumae, Shibuya-ku

When
10 am–4 pm weekends

Harritts Donuts

Who recommended
Kullen Ozeki

Why
All donuts should be this good

What to ask for
Sakura donut

Where
1-34-2 Uehara, Shibuya-ku

When
9.30 am—6 pm Wednesday—Friday,
11 am—6 pm Saturday, Sunday and
public holidays

Harritts Donuts takes the concept of the hidden Tokyo shop to ridiculously obscure levels.

Down a small side street is an old Japanese house, seemingly too small to house a cafe and donut factory; slide open the traditional wooden door and enter a cosy space, seating maybe ten people. The tiny venue is a perfect example of how well space is utilised in Tokyo.

Harritts' selection of donuts includes chocolate, cherry blossom, vanilla, earl grey, pumpkin and more. I don't like donuts as much as the next person, so when recommended that I go to this shop, I wasn't overly enthusiastic. I was very wrong. The donuts are a little denser and chewier than the more mass-produced varieties, and better for it. Their coffee is very high quality too. This is a great, secluded spot for a little down time in Tokyo, and a lesson on how the Japanese can take a thing and elevate it to perfection. In fact, Harritts do donuts so well, they now have stores in Taipei and Singapore.

Most places in Tokyo provide a challenge to shoot due to their size, but Harritts takes the cake, particularly at full capacity.

Who recommended
Masahiro Onishi

Why
Cool, backstreet
Shibuya vibe

What to ask for
Coffee and French toast

Where
11-2 Udagawacho, Shibuya-ku

When
8 am–2 pm and 6 pm–midnight
(closed Monday and one Sunday
each month)

Bistro Rojiura

Bistro Rojiura is another great option for those looking for an early meal in a city not renowned for its breakfast.

And if the place reminds you a little of Path (see page 18), it's because it is owned by the same (small) restaurant group. A simple equation is in practice at Rojiura – good coffee, relaxing and comfortable decor, great food and informed service. But most of us know that simple doesn't mean easy. As with Path, there is great attention to detail in all aspects.

Again like Path, the venue has two personalities: the breakfast/brunch service is available until 2 pm, then the more serious dinner option begins at 6 pm. Breakfast is a tight menu – maybe granola with yoghurt, French toast, avocado with scrambled eggs, and a vegetable and lentil curry. The à la carte dinner menu is more extensive and ambitious, featuring carefully sourced meats and vegetables. There is also a set menu available at the ridiculously low price of 5400 yen. The wine list is mainly French small producers, with a bit of a lean towards the natural.

Rojiura may not be the true Japanese experience that many travellers to Tokyo are looking for (particularly those new to the city), but is loved by the urbane and international population living there.

43

Delifucious

Why
A seriously delicious
fish burger

What to ask for
Anago dog

Where
1-9-13 Higashiyama,
Meguro-ku

When
midday–9 pm
(closed Wednesday)

If this place was in the city where I live, there would be serious repercussions. This 'fast food' is what the Japanese do so well: replicate and innovate. Plus it's damn delicious.

Tokyo loves burgers, and there are great ones to be found in the city.

There's Henry's Burger, Blacows and Burger Mania, just to name a few. Obviously, Tokyo is a city that also loves its fish. It is highly fortunate that the man who decided it was time to unite the two was a sushi chef with ten years' experience in high-end restaurants; a man who knows how to buy fish and treat it well. (Sushi-chef-turned-sandwich-maker: it's the same back story as Camelback on page 14 – is this the start of a trend?) The resulting shop produces some of the tastiest burgers you are likely to find in the city, all happening to be of the fish variety.

The classic burger consists of a piece of pristine fish, bought from the market earlier that day, marinated in kombu seaweed, deep-fried and served with a coleslaw in a very light, fluffy bun with a tofu sauce. The textures and flavours are amazing. There are other burgers – crab croquette, horse mackerel, grilled fish.

Burgers aren't the only star. There is the anago (saltwater eel) hotdog, deep-fried and served with julienned cucumber and a thick dashi and soy glaze. If you need more fish, the fries are served with clam chowder sauce.

The interior of the shop has an edgy skater vibe about it, which matches the origins of its curious name – a portmanteau of 'fucking' and 'delicious'.

It's a unique concept, perfectly executed and with a real confidence about it. I can't help but think it is the start of something big.

Minatoya Takoyaki and Kakigori

The Sasazuka area is located just a short distance from well-known Shimokitazawa, and like many Tokyo train station locations, it has a pleasant village feel about it.

Lots of small bars and restaurants line its narrow streets, yet it doesn't have the crowds of Shimokitazawa or Shibuya.

Minatoya, down one of these small streets, is famous for its takoyaki and kakigori. Takoyaki, more commonly associated with the Kansai area of Japan (Osaka, Kyoto, Kobe, et al.), are pan-fried flour and octopus dumplings, topped with Japanese mayo, shaved bonito and ginger. Often served as street food, they come in many different textures, from slightly runny to almost soup. No matter their texture, you almost always burn your mouth on the first impatient bite.

Minatoya's version is as good as any, and their akashiyaki — a firmer, more eggy version of takoyaki — is equally good. However, the place is best known for the kakigori, a dessert concoction of shaved ice with various toppings.

If you've never had kakigori, and even if shaved-ice desserts don't generally appeal, I suggest you try Minatoya's. They converted me. The ice is very finely shaved to order and gently patted into a large ball, then garnished with the flavour of your choice. These change regularly, and all of the fruit purees are made in-house. Think rhubarb, nashi, persimmon, tiramisu and my absolute favourite, amazake (a thick, creamy, semi-fermented sweet rice drink, here served with a little sweet ginger).

Having lunch at a place like Minatoya, in an area like Sasazuka, gives you a great insight into how Tokyoites like to eat most of the time. Casual, inexpensive and delicious.

Who recommended
Hiroyasu Kawate

Why
A slice of suburban Tokyo life

What to ask for
Amazake kakigori

Where
2-41-20 Sasazuka,
Shibuya-ku

When
11 am–7 pm
(closed Wednesday)

Hiroyasu Kawate

Kawate comes from a family of chefs, including his father, brother and cousin. He felt that being a chef was his only real choice, but also the only one he desired, and Tokyo is the city he wanted to work in. Born and raised there, he loves the stimulation, creativity and inspiration that Tokyo offers.

At Kawate-san's stunning twenty-two-seater Florilege in Aoyama (2-5-4 Jingumae, Shibuya-ku; midday–3.30 pm and 6.30–11 pm; closed Wednesday), the dining room and kitchen are almost one and the same. Diners sit at a counter set slightly above the kitchen, looking down on the action. The kitchen is not like a stage; it is a stage. The chefs literally have nowhere to hide. Watching their precise movements, the efficiency and economy of motion, and the subtle, often non-verbal communication between them, is a real joy. It adds so much to the dining experience.

At the centre of all this activity is Kawate-san – focused and intense, but always enjoying himself.

His food is often described as French, but you would never see this style of food in France – it could only happen in Japan, and in particular Tokyo. This is not just because Kawate uses only Japanese produce. The distinction also lies in his aesthetic – his plating is sparse and elegant, and the dishes themselves are equally restrained.

Florilege has been in its current location for about three years, and in that time I have seen Kawate grow from a great chef to a great restaurateur. He is aware, as all great chef-restaurateurs are, of the importance of the whole dining experience, of which the food is but a part. Dining at Florilege is an event, a moment when you lose yourself in the complete immersive experience that a great restaurant can offer.

The wait at this coffee house was long enough to read a book — he wasn't the only one doing so either!

Koffee Mameya

Omotesando Koffee was a fabled coffee shop in Tokyo that is still talked about today.

It started as a pop-up located in a *back* backstreet of Omotesando, in a traditional Japanese house with a starkly minimalist, geometric interior. The coffee was brewed in an equally precise manner. Even the pastries sold there were perfect cubes. It was devastating news to many when the shop closed after about four years of operation.

But just one year later it was reborn, in the same location but a new building (the previous building was pulled down), with the new name of Koffee Mameya.

Mameya is possibly even more purist in its offerings. The new building is clad in wood-panelling charred by an ancient Japanese technique that is having a resurgence, called yakisugi, which gives the building a look older than its years. The interior is almost like an old apothecary — the coffee arranged on the shelf the medicine that will cure your ills. Two baristas wear pale-blue overcoats. You approach the counter and they offer you the menu, consisting of up to twenty-five different roasts from up to five different roasters, with the coffees arranged by roasting from light to dark.

Mameya have chosen not to roast their own beans — they feel their strength is to create the best coffee they can from the best sourced beans.

Don't come here looking for a latte: this is a milk-free zone, with the coffee made via espresso and, more commonly, via pour-over. Also don't come here looking for a seat or a place to hang around for a chat. This cafe is a singular vision from owner Eiichi Kunitomo — a place where coffee making is elevated to art, and the drink itself gets the reverence usually applied to wine or whisky.

To some urbane Tokyoites, Koffee Mameya is seen as a venue more for tourists than locals, but if that is the case, tourists are the winners here.

Why
Coffee in its purest form

What to ask for
Pour-over

Where
4-15-3 Jingumae, Shibuya-ku

When
10 am–6 pm daily

KOFFEE MAMEYA

Kitchen Town

For anyone even vaguely interested in cooking, Kappabashi-dori, or Kitchen Town, is a must.

The street is not overly long, but densely packed with stores selling all things cooking- and restaurant-related, and you should allow a good few hours for exploration. Located in Matsugaya, Taito, most of the shops are open Monday to Saturday.

Crockery shops are the most prominent on the street, with plates at very cheap prices. Just remember that once you put the freight on top to get them back home, prices usually become comparable to home.

The stores selling kitchen gadgets, pots, pans, spoons and similar paraphernalia are worth digging through (and it's generally an easier task fitting these in your luggage).

Many shops specialise in a certain product, such as the Kanaya Brush store. Soft pastry brushes, hard scrubbing brushes, art brushes, handmade toothbrushes, make-up brushes – if brushes are your thing (and really, who isn't into some form of brush?) this is the place for you. The stunning handmade straw brooms can set you back around 20,000 yen.

If you are a freak for coffee gear, Union Coffee is where you will want to spend your time.

A number of stores specialise in plastic replica food, always a popular souvenir. These items are generally handmade, so don't go expecting a bargain. One store, Ganso Shokuhin Sample-ya, even offers classes on making your own.

My all-time favourite store is Kama Asa with their extensive range of Japanese charcoal grills, from tiny one-person grills, right through to grills large enough for restaurants. I always spend too long in here.

Kappabashi-dori is a fascinating strip, and while it does have an element of tourism to it, it is still used and frequented by the local restaurant industry.

Uoriki

**One of the great pleasures of a trip to Tokyo
is visiting the depachika, or food halls,
on the basement floor of department stores.**

Ginza has good ones, particularly Mitsukoshi. Isetan in Shinjuku is more upmarket, home to patissiers from around the world. Takashimaya, also in Shinjuku, has everything you would ever need. Tokyu Food Show in Shibuya may be a little less well presented, but also has a great selection.

Tokyu's Uoriki Sushi are fish wholesalers and retailers, so to say they know fish is quite the understatement. They have a number of sushi stores scattered around the city. At Tokyu they have seating for around ten people, mostly at the bar, and the turnover of seats is fast.

Visitors to Tokyo often think sushi is a regular meal for the Japanese – an everyday food. This is not the case. But when the Japanese do eat sushi, more often than not it's from one of the country's more affordable sushi chains. At Uoriki, don't expect sushi that is exotic or highly crafted, but sushi that is extremely fresh and ridiculously cheap. The chirashi don, or scattered sushi on rice, usually includes calamari, mackerel, salmon, tuna, prawns, salmon roe and snapper, all for well under 2000 yen. Uoriki is the sort of lunch stop that's ideal when you're on the go – but it is so good, you may plan your next day with the same stop in mind.

Who recommended
Kan Morieda

Why
The cheapest way
to eat quality sushi

What to ask for
Chirashi don

Where
Tokyu Department Store,
2-24-1 Shibuya, Shibuya-ku

When
10 am–9 pm daily

Anis

___

Who recommended
Zaiyu Hasegawa and
Hiroyasu Kawate

Why
Expertly cooked game

What to ask for
A counter seat to watch
the chef in action

Where
1-9-7 Hatsudai, Shibuya-ku

When
11.30 am–2.30 pm
and 6 pm–11.30 pm
(closed Monday and the second
Sunday of the month)

Chef Susumu Shimizu and his restaurant Anis made for one of the more inspiring experiences on a recent trip to Tokyo.

His restaurant, in a small backstreet of Hatsudai, Shibuya, is unassuming on the outside, warm and comforting on the inside. Nothing in its appearance informs you that you're about to have a meal cooked by one of the most skilled in the field, and to dine from a menu specialising in game. On the day we visited, Shimizu-san was the sole staff member present. As well as attending to the many pots on the stove and to the meats grilling, he was serving drinks and attending to guests, all with a deft hand.

Shimizu-san has a great resume including stints in France at Arpège, and at La Maison des Bois – Marc Veyrat, and it shows in his technique. Every movement is precise, almost choreographed. He knows the dimensions of every part of his kitchen and looks as if he could work blindfolded. It is a pleasure to watch him at work.

At Anis, Shimizu-san has created his own style of cooking. All his meats are cooked on the plancha (the Spanish word for the flat-topped grill), which takes pride of place in the centre of a very open kitchen. Meats are cooked as large joints, or whole in the case of birds. Guinea fowls stand upright on their legs, cooking slowly. The process takes many hours and results in perfectly cooked, moist birds – the best guinea fowl I have ever eaten.

We also enjoyed pigeon with puntarella (a variety of chicory), abalone with smoked potato, wild boar with red cabbage and salsify, lightly smoked duck with turnips, and the biggest surprise of all (at least for us) – the hiyodori. Hiyodori, or brown-eared bulbul, is a tiny bird native to eastern Asia. It was cooked whole with its innards intact, and served with oranges, which are one of its food sources; it was surprisingly gamey for such a small bird, the bitterness of the innards adding to its complexity. Our whole meal was balanced with a judicial use of vegetables, and a salad of bitter leaves at the end.

Shimizu-san is a tour de force of a chef and his food served at Anis is exceedingly delicious.

Shimizu-san finishing a
sauce that perfumed the
room with the most earthy
aromas. The level of
precision and timing required
would be invisible to the
untrained eye.

Gris

Who recommended
Kullen Ozeki

Why
Experience one of Tokyo's
creative young chefs

What to ask for
Set menu plus matching drinks

Where
1-35-3 Uehara, Shibuya-ku

When
Midday–1.30 pm
weekends and public holidays;
6–9 pm daily

**An exciting number of young chefs are
arriving on the scene in Tokyo,
and Shusaku Toba is one of the best.**

His food is modern and international in aesthetic, with Japanese
influences through the produce and technique, giving his menus
a sense of place.

Gris has twenty seats, making it fairly large by Tokyo standards. Its
modern decor matches Shusaku's creative and beautifully plated food.
The dishes on offer may be mackerel with quinoa cooked in beetroot,
a fried oyster with yurine (lily bulb) and calamansi (South-East Asian
lime), or delicate potato gnocchi made from overwintered potatoes
and served with karasumi (salted mullet roe).

The lunch tasting menu is one of Tokyo's true bargains: 7000 yen for
nine courses. The wine service is well informed, with a lean towards
the natural and to more idiosyncratic producers. Unusually for Tokyo,
there is a printed list of wines offered by the glass, which makes things
so much easier (at many other restaurants, asking about wines by the
glass will see a waiter bringing all the available bottles to your table).
The interesting drinks list also has a great selection of craft beers and
sake, including a Heiwa pale ale from a sake producer in Wakayama
and the unique Daigo No Shizuku sake from Terada Honke.

When dining at Gris, you can't help but be thrilled to see what the new
generation of chefs like Shusaku are producing, and to feel you are part
of a changing of the guard in Tokyo's dining scene.

Meikyoku Kissa Lion

'Meikyoku kissa' is the name given to classical music cafes in Japan.

These venues date back to a time when a personal turntable was a luxury, and people would go out to listen to music in a shared environment.

'Shared' rather than 'social', as these cafes generally weren't (and still aren't) places for conversation. Orders with the waiter are made in hushed tones, and conversations between customers, if they must happen at all, are expected to be at similar levels.

Meikyoku Kissa Lion is one of the oldest and most famous of the remaining music cafes. It is located in Dogenzaka, an area that became known for its love hotels and nightclubs. Built in 1926, destroyed in World War II and then rebuilt, the cafe is a small glimpse of old Tokyo. The building itself looks even older than its years – baroque with an air of decay about it.

The interior is all velvet, hidden corners, ornamentation, creaky floorboards with a covering of worn marmoleum. The seating is arranged like a theatre, facing forwards towards what is essentially a stage with a number of turntables. Behind these turntables are well over 5000 vinyl records, and behind them is the centrepiece: two beautiful, towering wooden speakers, providing a '3D sound environment', or so it says on the speakers. They do produce an amazing sound, one that you can feel inside yourself. As a record finishes and another is placed on the turntable, the staff member in charge makes a quiet announcement with the name of the record.

You don't really go for the quality of the coffee, but Meikyoku Kissa Lion is so unique that you can't help but grin like a fool when you are here. It's magical, even. But you must follow the rules: don't go with a large group (in fact, the place is probably best enjoyed on your own), and respect the space. Along with the Japanese garden at the Nezu Museum in Minami-Aoyama, this is one of my favourite places to have a little down time in the middle of a busy Tokyo day.

'No photos allowed.'
'Quiet please.' I could
have photographed here
for hours; instead, just
two images were captured.

Who recommended
Robbie Swinnerton

Why
An experience that could
really only happen in Tokyo

What to ask for
A table up front,
close to the speakers

Where
2-19-13 Dogenzaka,
Shibuya-ku

When
11 am–10.30 pm daily

Saikoro

There are thousands of ramen joints in Tokyo, many of them good, a number of them great.

Choosing which one to go to often comes down to location – because when there's so much of a good thing on offer, a restaurant needs to be very good indeed to get you travelling out of your way. Saikoro in Nakano is a good reason for an excursion, even if just a small one (it's only a short ride on the Chuo line from Shinjuku station).

Confusingly, the shop has the name 'Jiraigen' in neon out the front (the name of its parent company). Inside, Saikoro has a 1950s diner feel – checkerboard tiles, black laminex bar, round chrome bar stools. The music runs from J-pop to '50s rockabilly, to '80s funk. The service, as in any good ramen place, is quick and efficient. The three-person team (one cook, one facilitator, one host) moves with a seamlessness that only comes from doing the same job for a long time.

Saikoro are famous for their niboshi/shoyu broth. Niboshi are dried sardines, and the resulting dashi made from them is stronger and more robust than the better-known bonito dashi. Saikoro's version is rich and complex with a hint of chilli. You can see the stock boiling in enormous pots at the back of the kitchen as you sit at the bar.

The chashu, or braised pork that is served with ramen, is equally delicious, and moister than most chashu encountered.

The toughest choice you have is deciding between the ramen and tsukemen styles. The ramen is satisfying in a way that only a bowl of rich broth with noodles can be, but the tsukemen – where the noodles are served chilled on the side, and the broth is thicker and richer for dipping – is so delicious, and has the added bonus of the extra texture in the noodles. Perhaps use the weather as your guide: tsukemen is certainly more popular in the warm summer months, whereas a bowl of steaming noodles in broth is perfect in the middle of a Tokyo winter. 'Saikoro' means dice in Japanese, but there is no gamble with the ramen here – excellent no matter which bowl you choose.

Why
No ramen, no life

What to ask for
Help with the ordering
vending machine

Where
2-28-8 Nakano, Nakano-ku

When
11 am–2.30 am
Monday–Saturday,
11 am–11 pm
Sunday and public holidays

79

Sakurai Tea Experience

Why
A modern take on the
tea ceremony

What to ask for
Gyokuro

Where
5-6-23 Minami-Aoyama,
Minato-ku

When
11 am—11 pm weekdays,
11 am—8 pm weekends

This moment of the infusion
falling gracefully into the
delicate vessel is a reminder
of the magic that happens
when you just sit and observe.

This shop does what it says on the box: you don't come here just for a cup of tea, but to experience tea, albeit in a unique modern way.

Designed by the famed Shinichiro Ogata, the stylish and intimate interior takes its cues from traditional architecture and lays them over a minimalist aesthetic — all clean lines, no extraneous ornamentation, perfect functionality. It could exist nowhere else but in Japan, and is a must when visiting Tokyo.

The teas on offer cover all the well-known Japanese styles, and some that may be less familiar. Sencha (green leaf tea) is available of course, but also roasted green teas and fukamushicha (a green tea steamed longer during production to produce a sweet, less astringent brew with a bright colour).

Whenever we are here we can't help but have the gyokuro, considered to be the most luxurious of all green teas. The plants are shaded before harvest, creating greater levels of chlorophyll in the leaves and less bitterness. The tea is also much more savoury. Every time I've had the gyokuro at Sakurai, it has blown my mind with its intensity of flavour.

To prepare the tea, 10 g (¼ oz) of tea leaves are placed in a pot. For the first infusion, just 80 ml (2½ fl oz) of water at 40°C (105°F) is added, and the tea is allowed to steep for two minutes. The resulting extraction only consists of about a tablespoon, but it is the most intensely flavoured liquid you could imagine. Like a very savoury dashi broth, it is packed with umami. Further infusions are done with increasing water temperatures and volumes, creating different flavour profiles with each extraction. Then comes the real left-field finish, when the tea leaves are removed from the pot and served with a little salt and yuzu — delicious. It is a real pleasure watching the staff of Sakurai create your tea with choreographed elegance — it is not a 'tea ceremony', yet there is a great deal of ceremony.

The teas are served with wagashi, the traditional Japanese sweets that accompany tea. They are exceptional here, both exquisitely made and beautifully presented. Owner Shinya Sakurai previously worked at Higashiya, the renowned wagashi producer in Ginza.

If all the serenity and health-giving goodness of green tea is too much, there are tea cocktails available here too.

The level of detail here was completely at odds with the location. An urban haven full of revered Japanese craftsmanship.

Kagari

Why
Ramen doesn't really
get better than this

What to ask for
Tori paitan

Where
6-4-12 Ginza, Chuo-ku

When
10 am–10.30 pm daily

**If you were to eat only one bowl of ramen
in Tokyo (crazy thought, I know),
Kagari would be a very good choice.**

It has only been open about five years, in a number of different locations, but in that time has garnered a reputation for producing one of Tokyo's tastiest and more unique bowls of noodles.

They offer three choices: tori paitan, niboshi shoyu and tokusei tsukesoba.

The first is a chicken-based soup, rich and creamy from the chicken fat in the broth, with fine wheat noodles. It is like a chicken version of the classic pork tonkotsu, and may sound heavy but is actually quite light, yet with an intense chicken flavour.

The second option is a rich, salty broth made from niboshi (dried sardines) and seasoned with shoyu (soy sauce), with the same noodles.

The third option is their tsukemen ramen. In this dish the noodles are served cold and separate from the broth, the idea being that the noodles don't overcook sitting in the hot broth. Kagari's tsukemen is perfectly executed. Tsukemen noodles give you a real textural bite, and the rich broth is thicker, so the broth sticks to the noodles as you dip them in.

The popularity of Kagari comes with a cost – not in money but in time. There is never not a queue out the front, with varying wait times depending on the time of the day, ranging from twenty to thirty minutes to well over an hour. The place only seats eight, but the queue does progress quickly.

Keep this in mind when you finally get your seat at the counter. This is not a place to linger over your bowl of noodles, or for casual conversation, or scrolling through your social media feeds. This is a place to eat your noodles and get out – then contemplate the magnificence of the ramen on your way back to the subway.

Kan Morieda

I first met Kan at his wonderfully idiosyncratic restaurant, Salmon and Trout (4-42-7 Daizawa, Setagaya-ku; 6–10 pm Thursday–Monday). The place is part bicycle shop, part cosy dining room, and don't expect to see any salmon or trout on the menu. Kan produces creative, sometimes edgy, always delicious dishes from his tiny kitchen. Looking like a Japanese Harry Potter, his infectious, cheeky character shines from behind the counter. He is genuinely happy to be cooking for you.

The other place where I have seen Kan look truly at home is at the UNU Farmers' Market (see page 35). He knows all the stallholders, and everyone knows him. It is his playground.

The food that Kan produces reflects his work history, including the modern style of the Tapas Molecular Bar at Tokyo's Mandarin Oriental Hotel, the international style of Tetsuya's in Sydney, and the traditional Japanese of Kogetsu in the Tokyo neighbourhood of Aoyama. He uses all of these influences, plus his interest in South-East Asian cuisine, to create his own style, unbounded by borders or norms. Many chefs can't pull off this free-ranging approach, but Kan's sympathy and respect for the cuisines and styles he borrows from brings it all together.

The other thing about Kan is his seemingly endless energy. He always seems to have his finger in some other project, while working the pass at Salmon and Trout five nights a week. Other involvements include a lemon sour bar in the Golden Gai (the small jumble of bars in an old part of Shinjuku that miraculously survived the events of the twentieth century), a grilled mackerel restaurant, a fruit syrup bar, a barbecue izakaya, and a number of magazines. He is the sort of person who needs to be busy, and achieves this spectacularly.

Nishiya Coffee House

**This coffee house is almost the antithesis
of the cool, minimal, hipster coffee joints that
normally get all the limelight.**

Inspired by the coffee shops of Italy, owner Kyohei Nishiya has gone
for a feeling of warmth and elegance – a white-tiled exterior with
blue-and-white striped awnings, and inside: warm wood-panelling with
a large burnished aluminium and timber bar, the espresso machine
framed like a Japanese temple by the shelves around it. This is a
comfortable and grounded place, and feels like it has been here much
longer than its five years.

Obviously you come here for coffee, and they do excellent espresso
covering all bases, e.g. latte, cappuccino, macchiato. They also have
a small selection of well-made cafe dishes to enjoy alongside.
The custard purin (pudding) is a must. The espresso banana shake,
while not my thing, has built its own fan base, and if you are looking
for something savoury, their version of croque monsieur is good.

Wandering around Tokyo is exhausting; you end up walking a lot,
and this is a perfect place to break up the day, relax, and spend a few
moments people-watching.

Who recommended
Kan Morieda

Why
Great place for a pit stop

What to ask for
Custard purin

Where
1-4-1 Higashi, Shibuya-ku

When
11 am—7 pm (closed Tuesday)

Gen Gen An

This is one of those lucky discoveries that happen every time we go to Tokyo.

They usually occur on the walk to or from a lunch or dinner destination, when we wander down some side street, some back alley. We find a place we didn't know we wanted to find, until we came across it.

So, wandering back from a lunch featuring too much booze, and not looking for any more of it, we came across Gen Gen An, and it was exactly what we needed.

The small shop specialises in tea. They offer an extensive range including sencha (green leaf tea), hojicha and kamairicha (roasted green teas), and black teas. There is also the option of green tea or hojicha lattes, if that sort of thing floats your boat.

Tea preparation here is a serious business — methodical, not speedy, very precise. The resulting teas are delicious. And it turns out that Gen Gen An also offers tea cocktails (we had more booze, after all).

The iced teas, including senchas infused with yuzu or lemongrass, are particularly good, especially when the weather is warm.

The place itself is cool. One wall is decorated with hundreds of cassette tapes like a mosaic, and music is played from a giant boom box. Cassettes are back, baby.

Why
Excellent tea in a
casual environment

What to ask for
Iced tea

Where
4-8 Udagawacho, Shibuya-ku

When
11 am–7 pm Sunday,
Tuesday, Wednesday;
11 am–11 pm Thursday–Saturday

Tokyo Vinyl

For me, the main attraction of going to Tokyo is the food.

But you can't eat all day, or at least not all day every day, and other distractions are needed. Tokyo's record stores are a big one. The stores range from specialist places to those spanning many genres of music; whichever you visit, you need to put in the time to get the rewards.

Shinjuku has many stores, and one of the more specialised is Dub Store (7-13-5 Nishi-Shinjuku, Shinjuku-ku; midday–8 pm daily). This smaller shop focuses solely on Jamaican music, particularly from the 1960s through to the early '80s. Think reggae (obviously), but also dub, ska, jazz, et al. Dub Store is now pressing their own vinyl, reissuing old recordings.

The biggest store in Shinjuku is Disk Union (3-31-4 Shinjuku, Shinjuku-ku; 11 am–9 pm daily); they also have other branches in Shibuya and Ochanomizu. In fact, Disk Union Shinjuku is spread over six separate stores. The main store is eight storeys high with each floor dedicated to a genre, starting in the basement with J-pop and moving up the floors to prog rock, world music, '80s rock and punk/hardcore. A whole floor is dedicated to CDs; in fact, in 2014 it was reported that 85 per cent of all music sold in Japan was on CD, despite the rest of the world turning to digital.

Another great area for vinyl discoveries is Koenji, which is a place worth heading to for many reasons. The punk movement in Tokyo was born there, and there are still remnants of those times in the feel of the place. It is edgy, very cool – but a little more mature than some of Tokyo's other subculture districts. There are more vinyl stores in Koenji than you could visit in a day, but must-visits are Be-In Records (3-57-8 Koenji-Minami, Suginami-ku; 12.30–8.30 pm daily), Enban (3-59-11 Koenji-Minami, Suginami-ku; 1–8 pm daily) and EAD Records (4-28-13 Koenji-Minami, Suginami-ku; 1–9 pm Wednesday–Monday). Koenji is also home to some of Tokyo's best second-hand clothing stores and if this is your scene, you should plan a full day in Koenji at least.

Wineshop Flow

Why
One of Tokyo's best bottle shops

What to ask for
Advice from the knowledgeable
and passionate owner

Where
2-28-3 Nishihara, Shibuya-ku

When
3 pm–midnight Monday–Saturday,
3–8 pm Sunday

**Down Nishihara Street in Hatagaya is
the sort of bottle shop and wine bar that you
want around the corner from home.**

Hatagaya is an up-and-coming neighbourhood with just enough shops, cafes, restaurants and bars to make it interesting. While only a short distance from Shibuya, it is a world away from the pace and bright lights – the sort of place I would choose to live in Tokyo (though I'd spend far too much time at Wineshop Flow).

You enter down some stairs, emerging into a space that looks like the inside of a wine barrel. The whole shop is lined with cedar; its woody, sweet smell can be detected immediately. You enter the retail part of the shop through a dramatic Chinese-style moon gate, constructed from more cedar. The whole room is climate-controlled (I imagine people would spend a long time making their choice here on a hot summer day), and the wine selection has to be one of the best in Tokyo.

The bar at the front of the shop is a casual, comfortable space to work through the small but interesting selection of craft beer, cider, and wine solely of the lo-fi variety, from Europe, the United States, Japan and Australia. The food on offer is simple, effective snacks – nuts, charcuterie, cheese.

Owner Kenko Fukagawa is a serious audiophile, and the back of the bar is littered with amps, CD players and, of course, turntables. Alt-folk tunes fill the space but never drown out conversation.

This is a shrine to natural wine and to craftsmanship, both integrating seamlessly.

Fuglen is gorgeous inside and out, and the buzz and activity is infinite.

Fuglen

Fuglen is a cafe and coffee roaster hailing from Oslo, Norway; however, it fits so seamlessly into Tokyo you would think it is home-grown.

The original outpost of this part coffee house, part cocktail lounge is located in a quiet backstreet in Tomigaya, an up-and-coming district of Shibuya. (They have recently opened a second branch in Asakusa.) The aesthetic matches the multi-personality approach – a bit tiki bar, a bit beach house, with modernist furniture and fittings throughout.

Fuglen focuses on its coffee persona during the day, selling very good espresso. You can sit at the bar or on one of the lounges, or even outdoors, and watch Tokyo's expat community plus a good percentage of Japanese utilise the space as a meeting point, temporary office and caffeine pit stop on the way to and from work. The crowd leans towards creatives, drawn there by the design of the place. (The company behind Fuglen has a design studio called Norwegian Icons a couple of buildings up the street.)

You can get a beer or wine during the day, but if you are after a cocktail, you need to wait until 7 pm when the place officially flips over to a cocktail bar. Cocktails are classic varieties with small twists to give them a sense of place. The Scandinavian negroni is fabulous – a mixture of Aalborg aquavit, Antica Formula vermouth, Gran Classico, Abbott's bitters and grapefruit zest.

If you want food alongside your drinks, then Fuglen only has limited offerings – muesli in the mornings, open sandwiches later on – but you are welcome to bring your own food.

Sitting outside on a summer night drinking one of Fuglen's fine cocktails has to be one of Tokyo's more cosmopolitan experiences.

Who recommended
Robbie Swinnerton

Why
Great coffee, cocktails and vibe

What to ask for
Scandinavian negroni

Where
1-16-11 Tomigaya, Shibuya-ku

When
8 am–10 pm Monday and Tuesday,
8 am midnight Wednesday,
8 am–1 am Thursday,
8 am–2 am Friday, 9 am–2 am Saturday,
9 am–midnight Sunday

Mikkeller

Mikkeller, the gypsy brewing company from Denmark, opened their first store in Tokyo in 2015.

It was a short-lived affair, to the disappointment of many, but was to re-emerge in a new location one year later.

And it is a great new location, down a backstreet of Dogenzaka, an area once regarded as somewhat seedy with its proliferation of love hotels, but which is slowly being reborn. Mikkeller is opposite a temple, and down the street you'll also find Meikyoku Kissa Lion, a place that couldn't be more different (see page 7).

Mikkeller is all bare concrete and pale wood, minimalist and functional in design. The main function is beer drinking and socialising. There is plenty of standing room between the few bar tables downstairs, with some concrete seats on the window ledge. Upstairs are a few more tables for those wanting a seat.

Those window seats are a pleasant place on a sunny afternoon to partake in one of Mikkeller's twenty beers on tap. The selection – about half Mikkeller's own brands, half Japanese craft beers – is well curated with a good cross-section of styles, from pales and IPAs, wheat beers and sours, to some more experimental brews.

While the afternoons are relaxed, nights are another story. The place gets busy and is all the more fun for it. A simple menu with open sandwiches and meatballs is on offer to balance out your alcohol intake.

One thing to note, however: this place shows how the Japanese can perfect anything, even the disinterested hipster service done so well in the West.

Who recommended
Kan Morieda

Why
Craft beer in a buzzy
contemporary space

What to ask for
Mikkeller's sour beers are
always good

Where
2-19-11 Dogenzaka,
Shibuya-ku

When
3 pm–12.30 am Monday–Thursday,
3 pm–1.30 am Friday,
midday–1.30 am Saturday,
midday–12.30 am Sunday
and public holidays

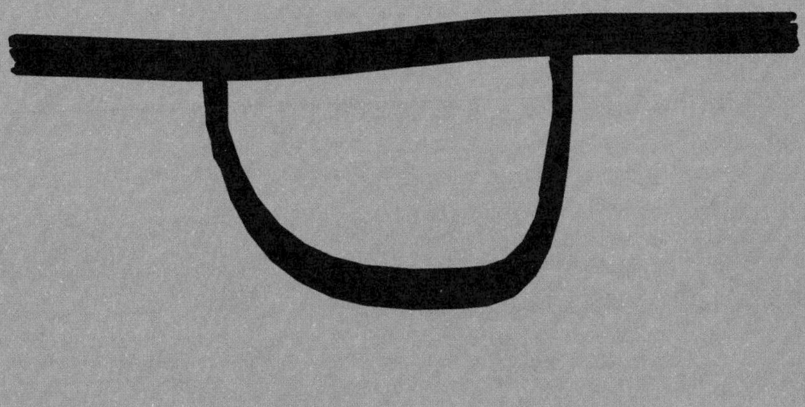

Hakkoku

Why
Cutting-edge sushi in a
friendly atmosphere

What to ask for
A booking (the menu is set)

Where
3rd floor, 6-7-6 Ginza, Chuo-ku

When
11.30 am–2 pm and
5–11 pm (closed Sunday)

Each service here is a performance.
 The place is very serious but
the people who work here aren't!
Their generosity of spirit was a
beautiful thing.

I first had Hiroyuki Sato's sushi at Tokami, the sushi restaurant where he received his first Michelin star.

I remember the meal being striking for a number of reasons, including Sato-san's open and friendly manner, his amazing tuna, and his sole use of red vinegar in his shari, or sushi rice.

He left Tokami in 2017 and has now opened his own restaurant, Hakkoku. As good as Tokami was, Hakkoku is another big step up.

The restaurant is singular in having no otsumami. Otsumami are the snacks or appetisers often served before and during a sushi meal, usually including a couple of vegetable dishes, and tending to be low-key so as not to take any attention away from the sushi. Here, however, sushi is the only star.

The meal is a progression of thirty pieces of nigiri and maki sushi – or twenty-two pieces at lunch. (Nigiri is moulded rice with a topping, while maki is wrapped in seaweed.) I discovered thirty pieces of sushi is just slightly over my quota – it can be very filling.

There is a strong emphasis on tuna, but the selection is also driven by seasonality. At the time of my meal at Hakkoku, it was peak squid season, and there were at least three types served.

I enjoy Sato-san's shari for its stronger flavour and distinct lack of sweetness (there is no sugar at all). He uses aged red vinegar made from sake lees, which works particularly well with oily, rich fish. Whether the full-bodied flavour works as well with lighter fish depends on your personal preference.

The restaurant is divided into three spaces, each seating six people. This is large for a sushi restaurant, but with an individual preparation area attached to each space, Hakkoku remains intimate. Sato-san makes sushi in one area, and his sous-chef makes it in another (the third area wasn't operating the day I visited). Seats with Sato-san himself are booked up and hard to come by, but his sous-chef is accomplished and engaging, and speaks good English, which is helpful.

You can't help but feel that Hakkoku is pushing at the boundaries of the confined and conservative sushi world. The chefs achieve being both extremely focused and friendly, and the decor of the place has a modern feel. There are female and Western staff on the floor, and other small touches like napkins at the table. Dining at Hakkoku goes above and beyond exceptional sushi.

Another 8

In a city the size of Tokyo, almost every scene is well represented, with craft beer no exception.

A handful of new beer venues seem to open each time I visit, and one of the recent additions is Another 8 in Meguro.

The original store is in Kyoto, called Before 9 – I'd been there and liked its style and substance a lot, so a visit to the Tokyo store seemed a good idea. Another 8 is located in a fairly unremarkable part of Meguro, which makes its stylish interior all the more striking and unexpected. And while it may be minimalist in style, it is a very functional and quite comfortable space. The vibe is relaxed and the crowd mixed, but with a definite leaning towards the younger demographic.

Eight beers are offered on tap, which included a mix of Japanese and imported (mainly American) beers the night I was there. Japanese craft beer is currently on a steep learning curve, and there is plenty of good mixed in with the bad. Another 8 do a great job of curating their selection, and they also have a small but good selection of sake available if beer is not your thing.

The food on offer is of a higher standard than at most other beer venues. Dishes like bagna cauda (anchovy and garlic dip) with sparklingly fresh raw vegetables, potato salad with smoked egg, or marinated octopus and celery are perfect beer matches.

If you are after the ideal double bill, Another 8 is just around the corner from Tonki, one of Tokyo's best tonkatsu – crumbed pork – restaurants (1-1-2 Shimomeguro, Meguro-ku; 4–10.45 pm Wednesday–Monday except third Monday of the month).

Why
See where Japanese
craft beer is headed

What to ask for
Bagna cauda alongside your beer

Where
1-2-18 Shimomeguro, Meguro-ku

When
5 pm–1 am daily

Toriyoshi

While I'm sure you're never more than a short walk away from a yakitori restaurant in Tokyo, it's good to have your favourites.

I have a number of go-to yakitori up my sleeve. Toriyoshi is one, and, although slightly more upmarket than many other yakitori places, it still has a great neighbourhood atmosphere, with that feeling that many of its customers are regulars.

The place opens late afternoon and is busy from the get-go. The early evening crowd is full of people just out of work looking for a snack and a drink; the drinks flow steadily.

There is an English menu here, but with all the skewers in a glass display cabinet, you can also just point and wait. Unlike many yakitori venues, there is a strong emphasis on vegetables, and these skewers are as good as the essential skewered bird. They might include bamboo shoots, tiny shishito peppers, gingko nuts and, if you happen to be there at the right time of year, sansai (mountain vegetables).

The chicken skewers are the real star. It is at yakitori restaurants where many visitors first discover that the Japanese are masters of nose-to-tail eating, and the skewer where it all comes together is known as the chochin, consisting of meat, liver and an egg removed from a bird before the shell has fully formed.

The beauty of yakitori is that you can either play it safe and go for morefamiliar cuts of meat for a tasty meal, or you can stretch your boundaries and go for the 'variety' options – eat this way and your meal can be a revelation.

Toriyoshi doesn't take bookings, so it's a matter of turning up and hoping for the best. It's best to avoid peak dinner times. You may have to wait, but it is always worth it.

Why
Yakitori that is refined but still fun

What to ask for
Chochin skewer

Where
2-8-6 Kamimeguro, Meguro-ku

When
5–11 pm weekdays,
3.30–11 pm weekends

Ippo

Who recommended
Melinda Joe

Why
A classic izakaya with great fish dishes

What to ask for
Horse mackerel with shiso,
leek and ginger

Where
2nd floor, 1-22-10 Ebisu, Shibuya-ku

When
6 pm–midnight daily

An izakaya is usually described as the Japanese version of a pub.

However, I like to think of them as more like restaurants that have less emphasis on the niceties of dining, and more on the atmosphere and food. Tokyo's izakayas are generally hard to find and a little grimy around the edges, with a mix of customers from salarymen to creative types, older couples and younger groups. They have a good selection of booze, friendly service, and some of the tastiest food you can eat in the city. These are the kinds of places that Tokyoites frequent regularly.

Ippo is on the second floor of a nondescript building, its interior looking worn. While the place may seem less than exciting judging by appearances, the quality of the food on offer seals the deal.

The chefs behind the counter are convivial even when faced with language barriers from both sides. For those without a strong grasp of Japanese, the best option at almost any restaurant is to go for the omakase menu. This is a handy word to remember, essentially meaning a tasting menu that is based on the chef's whim. The only downside is that it is often assumed that foreigners will not want the more challenging dishes on offer. If you are interested in them, it is good to learn how to say 'I eat everything' – 'Nande mo tabemasu'. (A word of warning on dietary requirements: most places will be happy to cater to allergies, but through a mixture of language barriers and lack of exposure to customers with intolerances, it could be best to get something printed in Japanese to present at restaurants.)

The omakase menu at Ippo is just 2500 yen, fitting with another common theme among izakayas: dining at them is often very cheap. Most izakayas have a strong focus on seafood, but Ippo is all about seafood. Our meal started with mozuku seaweed, texturally challenging for many Western palates but delicious when you get used to it (slimy just isn't in the Western repertoire, but is very popular with Japanese, as evidenced by the fermented soy beans called natto).

Our sashimi was high quality and well presented. Following this we had tempura sakura ebi (tiny prawns named after cherry blossoms because of their colour, formed into fritters), tempura saltwater eel, and salmon jerky, all very fresh and tasty. A tartare of horse mackerel, chopped in front of us with two deba (traditional Japanese knives) and mixed with shiso, leek and ginger, was a real highlight. Ippo's food is all about quality produce prepared freshly and simply.

Masahiro
Onishi

Masahiro's path in coffee started as a passion, became an obsession, and is now a profession. While studying commerce and business at university, he began to get interested in the drink, working part-time as a barista. The moment came when he decided to see where coffee could really take him, and he travelled to one of the world's meccas of coffee – Melbourne. He worked there for a year, immersing himself in a scene that was vastly different from Tokyo's. Whereas Tokyo's coffee houses are generally small, catering to the neighbourhood market and producing a low number of carefully crafted cups, Melbourne's scene is much larger and busier, with many venues pulling thousands of cups a day.

Masahiro enjoyed working in this new atmosphere, but knew that when he returned to Japan, he would be happy to return to the realm of the smaller venue, making highly crafted, quality coffee. This is what he created with Switch. He opened his first store in fashionable Meguro (1-17-23 Meguro, Meguro-ku; 10 am–7 pm, closed Wednesday), just down from hipster central, Nakameguro. His second store is in equally cool Tomigaya (1-53-2 Tomigaya, Shibuya-ku; 8 am–8 pm weekdays, 10 am–7 pm weekends). Both areas have an urbane residential vibe that suited Masahiro's desire to create that perfect neighbourhood coffee shop; the kind of place locals would visit daily. However, word soon filtered out and his stores have become destinations for people from elsewhere.

Switch roasts all their beans in-house, with four varieties for espresso. They also offer pour-over and filter coffee, and serve an espresso and tonic, a drink people either love or hate.

Masahiro loves what he does, and it shows in the attention to detail and perfection that Switch strives for in every cup.

Kome Kome

Who recommended
Masahiro Onishi

Why
An intimate sake experience

What to ask for
Let Naoki guide you

Where
4-12-13 Meguro, Meguro-ku

When
6 pm–midnight Monday,
Wednesday–Saturday;
3–10 pm Sunday and public holidays

Kome Kome is the type of place you always hope to find in Tokyo.

A tiny, cosy sake bar run by a passionate, idiosyncratic individual, who does it on their own terms — a place that makes you feel lucky to be part of it, even for just for a few hours.

Kome Kome has nine seats at a squeeze. Owner Naoki Fujita is the sole staff member, and his knowledge of sake, or rather, nihonshu, is extensive. (In Japanese, 'sake' means all alcoholic beverages in general, while 'nihonshu' refers specifically to the rice wine that most non-Japanese call sake.) Naoki will happily guide you through his favourite varieties, serving them at different temperatures to suit each drink.

The food served out of his small kitchen is exactly what you want with sake — simple, tasty dishes with a strong emphasis on vegetables and fish. If available, the bukkake rice (rice with broth poured over the top) is a great way to finish a meal.

As a bonus, Kome Kome is literally just around the corner from Kabi (see page 17), and the two make a great double act.

Kome Kome is the benchmark for what a one-person operation should be, and Naoki says it all through his gentle face.

Kokoromai

Who recommended
Makiko Iitsuka and
Kenichi Yamamoto

Why
Traditional Japanese meal
with rice as the hero

What to ask for
The set menu

Where
3-15-16 Shirokane, Minato-ku

When
6–11.30 pm
(closed Wednesday)

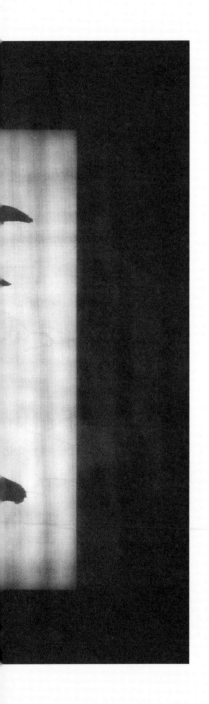

Kokoromai means 'heart of rice': fitting for a restaurant specialising in rice, but equally apt for a place with a lot of heart.

The restaurant has been around for over a decade and was recently taken over by a young husband-and-wife team, who are delightful and passionate hosts.

When ordering here, the first thing you must choose is the rice, even though it will be the last dish of the meal – traditionally in Japan the dishes preceding the rice are considered appetisers, and the rice the main event. There is usually a choice of eight rices ranging in variety and origin (though all Japanese, all white). If you go for the set omakase menu, you will be presented with two or three rices at the whim of the chef.

The meal follows a traditional format, though not so formalised or composed as kaiseki. A soup dish is followed by a selection of small dishes, then maybe a salad, some sashimi, a simmered fish dish, then a grilled dish (wagyu in our case). Finally, the rice course. A number of flavoursome toppings are served with the rice – chirimen (baby dried sardines), spicy mentaiko (pollock roe), ohitashi (dressed greens) and nori no tsukudani (seaweed cooked to a paste with soy and mirin).

There were noticeable textural differences between the rices, which are cooked and served in small earthenware pots (the long, slow cooking time is the reason you need to order the rice first). Make sure you dig down to the bottom of the pot where the rice forms a crunchy crust known as okoge, considered by many to be the best bit.

Of course, the best liquid accompaniment to a meal like this is the fermented rice beverage, sake. The food was truly delicious, with a wonderful lightness to it. Traditional and nourishing, with an insight into the importance of rice in Japanese culture.

Ayaka Makino

Tokyo is Ayaka's playground. She loves it for its diversity and activity, and especially for its food and drink.

Ayaka works hard, as most people do in hospitality. She has been a sommelier at some of Tokyo's best establishments, working with some of the world's most interesting wines. Ayaka has friends in many of Tokyo's great wine bars, cafes and restaurants, and gets around the city on her trusty old-school bike (one thing Ayaka dislikes about Tokyo is the crowded trains).

Before Tokyo, Ayaka worked in Nara, Kanazawa and her hometown of Shizuoka, and also worked for a year in Melbourne. I first met her when she was working at the very cool Path (see page 18), in the equally cool area of Tomigaya. Overseeing Path's wine program, she exuded the casual confidence of someone with plenty of knowledge of her subject, well beyond her years.

Ayaka is now at the very new, very exciting Inua, a restaurant established by ex-Noma chef Thomas Frebel (2-13-12 Fujimi, Chiyoda-ku; 5.30–10 pm Tuesday–Saturday).

Ayaka is Japanese, but oh-so Australian,
her warmth and attentiveness a
wonderful mix of the two cultures.

Ahiru Store

Who recommended
Ayaka Makino

Why
Hang with the wine cognoscenti

What to ask for
Octopus salad

Where
1-19-4 Tomigaya, Shibuya-ku

When
6 pm–midnight weekdays,
3–9 pm Saturday (closed first
Saturday of the month)

If I could have
a hole-in-the-wall, this
would be it. The buzz is
   palpable, the room so
alive. Quite possibly
   my favourite little bar
in Tokyo.

Deceptively, Ahiru Store is not a store, but one of Tokyo's favourite wine bars.

It beckons from the outside with its windows full of freshly made bread and wine bottles on display.

Ahiru Store focuses on biodynamic and organic wines, and also natural (or lo-fi) wines made with minimal intervention. The bar has been at the forefront of the natural wine movement in Tokyo since opening over a decade ago. The movement took off here even more than it did anywhere else, starting in the 1990s, and it shows no sign of slowing down, avoiding the short-lived trend cycle of the city. But no matter where you are in the world, natural wine is still a niche, and you need to know where to look. In Tokyo, Ahiru Store is your first and best choice.

The place is small — of course — with maybe eight seats at the bar, and standing room around some old barrels for about the same amount of people. Run by a brother and sister, it feels like one of those places that has always been there.

Sommelier Teruhiko Saito is one of the siblings and is passionate about the wines he serves. He certainly knows his stuff, although if your Japanese is not up to scratch, you may struggle to get to the depths of the wine list. Brush up on your natural wine knowledge, and go with your instincts. There is a good list of wines by the glass.

The food on offer fits the bar's ethos like a glove. The bread is made in-house and is fantastic (go for the grissini if it is available). A constant on the menu, and a must, is a salad of octopus, avocado and wasabi. Other dishes follow along the same lines of simple, fresh and tasty — think bonito carpaccio with pickled green peppers and ginger, or house-made sausages with mustardy potatoes.

The crowd is usually young, lively and friendly. The camaraderie may come from their bond of knowing they all managed to get a spot together in this popular bar. There are no bookings other than in the early evening before 6.30 pm, and queues start soon after. But once you are inside Ahiru Store, you may never want to leave.

Savoy Pizza and Pizza Studio Tamaki

Why
Pizza elevated

Savoy Pizza

What to ask for
Bianco pizza – not on the menu,
but available if you ask

Where
3-10-1 Motoazabu, Minato-ku

When
11.30 am–3 pm and
6–10.30 pm daily

Pizza Studio Tamaki

What to ask for
The Tamaki pizza

Where
1-24-6 Higashi-Azabu, Minato-ku

When
5–11 pm weekdays;
midday–4 pm and
5–10 pm weekends and
public holidays

Tokyo is a city where you can find the best of everything, though sometimes I'm still surprised by how good the food really is.

I had been hearing about some pizza places but had struggled to fit them in between the sushi, yakitori, sashimi, ramen, et al. However, on a recent trip I found myself dining at two pizza restaurants in one week.

Savoy Pizza has just eleven seats (and no bookings), with most seats on a bar overlooking the black steel wood-fired oven so you can watch the mesmerising skills of the chefs as they shape the pizza bases and top them with their small ingredient list. They only offer two pizzas — a margherita with mozzarella, tomato and basil, and a marinara with tomato, oregano and garlic. These are truly the best pizzas I have eaten. The flavours are fresh and vibrant and the dough is super delicious — both crusty and chewy with a wonderful smoky flavour. The dough is stored in old wooden boxes traditionally used for storing fish and is shaped by hand on a floured marble bench. The pizzas cook for just sixty seconds in the 480°C (895°F) oven.

There are some simple and very tasty dishes to have before your pizza or alongside, like tripe, marinated octopus, and bagna cauda (anchovy and garlic dip) with fresh vegetables. Wines and beers are there to help it all go down. The music played in the restaurant is eclectic, ranging from 1950s swing to '80s dag. I love this place.

Pizza Studio Tamaki is owned by chef Tsubasa Tamaki, whose long work history includes many of the best pizzerias in Tokyo (including Savoy). Where Savoy is all about minimalism, Studio Tamaki has a larger pizza selection — around ten or so — and also more antipasti. But the pizzas themselves remain minimalist masterpieces, where less is more and the total is greater than the sum of its parts.

The restaurant is a little larger than Savoy, with a number of high tables with bar stools, as well as stools around the kitchen (but again there is no option of booking). The gregarious front-of-house staff are good at turning the tables over and keeping the place buzzing all night.

Both restaurants show the ability of the Japanese to take a known product, study each element, and perfect every step, elevating it into a whole new realm. Pizza may not be on your list of must-dos in Tokyo, but it really should be. Of course, Tokyo is a city where double dinners are a thing, so these restaurants make a great pre-dinner dinner or post-dinner dinner.

Hiroo
Onogi

Who recommended
Melinda Joe

Why
Contemporary izakaya experience

What to ask for
Lobster rice hotpot

Where
2nd floor, 5-8-11 Hiro-o,
Shibuya-ku

When
6 pm–1 am weekdays,
6 pm–midnight Saturday

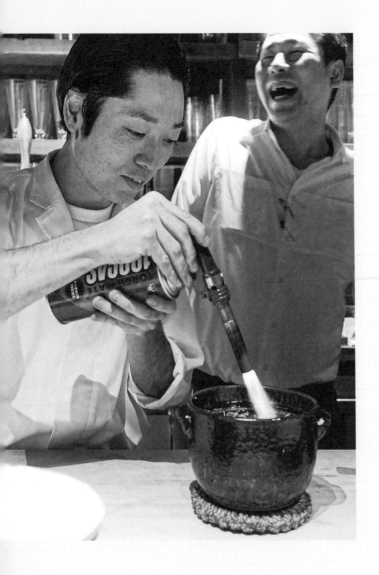

148

Hiroo Onogi is a venue that straddles the izakaya/restaurant border.

Like all good izakayas, it offers well-prepared food, great atmosphere and great sake, but in an environment that is much more refined than most. The room is beautiful – a balance between the industrial and the organic – with laid-back jazz playing over the sound system. The centrepiece is the base of a tree, including its complex root system, hanging from the ceiling.

Hiroo Onogi also deviates from a traditional izakaya in its more contemporary, creative food. Chef and owner Onogi-san cooks using traditional Japanese techniques but is happy to use non-Japanese ingredients. Entering the restaurant you notice a large display of vegetables. Onogi-san has good connections with a number of growers. As a chef I feel jealous whenever I see displays of Japanese vegetables – sure, we have great produce in Australia, but I have never seen the quality that exists in Japan.

As with many Japanese restaurants, the omakase menu, or set menu, remains the way to go here. (While Hiroo Onogi does have a large menu with an English version, it is always great to let the chef decide.)

Your meal could start with a delicate dish of sea urchin and crab with a vinegar jelly. Sashimi is a given and the quality here is high. (In actual fact, most sashimi I've eaten in Tokyo has been good to excellent. High-quality fish is readily available, and the quick turnover generally guarantees great sashimi in most places.)

After sashimi, the meal progresses through more fish and vegetable dishes, and usually a beef dish. The final course, a signature dish at Hiroo Onogi, is the lobster rice hotpot. On top of the steaming rice, a lobster head and claws are presented for your inspection. Then they are taken back by the chef, and you watch as he expertly removes and shreds the meat, folds it through the rice, and presents it back to you. As is the custom, you are offered seconds of this rice course, with the new rice roasted with a blowtorch to give it a different texture and flavour.

The meal is finished with monaka, a traditional Japanese sweet made of decorative rice wafers enclosing a flavoured filling, such as green tea, plus a pot of kuromame tea, a more unusual and delicious brew made of roasted black soy beans.

Isana Sushi Bar

Restaurants at the pointy end of Tokyo's sushi realm are expensive and notoriously difficult to get a booking at.

They offer memorable experiences where the performance of the chef is as important as the sushi presented. But in a city this size, there are always options to eat very well at a more moderate price. Isana Sushi Bar is one such place.

Run by the affable Junichi Onuki, Isana has a casual and personal air — something you don't often get in a sushi restaurant. Onuki-san speaks great English thanks to ten years working and making sushi in London, and he loves a chat. Ask him about the guitars decorating his space, and you'll learn of his love for the instrument and for American country artists Hank Williams and Johnny Cash.

The place is small, seating seven at the bar and another four at a table. The bar, as always, is where you want to be, to watch Onuki-san as he deftly prepares your fish.

While the meal is certainly focused on sushi, the courses preceding it can be equally interesting. Ours started with whelk (sea snail) cooked in dashi, monkfish liver terrine, and steamed octopus.

Sashimi followed, served piece by piece for truly enjoying the differences. Next came a rich piece of simmered buri (amberjack), then filefish with its liver, and bonito smoked with rice straw.

Then comes the sushi component of the meal. The shari, or rice, is flavoured with a mix of 30 per cent red vinegar and 70 per cent rice vinegar. (While there is a strong trend among Michelin-starred sushiya to use all red vinegar — an aged vinegar made from sake lees — Onuki-san finds this too aggressive.) Our sushi included ark clam, chutoro (medium-fatty tuna), prawn, red snapper and anago (saltwater eel). During proceedings we got a lesson on the history of edomae sushi, which is the Tokyo style of sushi (Edo being the city's old name).

The sushi here is high-end, yet a fraction of the price you pay at a Michelin-starred sushiya. The experience may not be as refined, but it has personality. This is the sushiya you want just around the corner from home.

Who recommended
Melinda Joe

Why
High-end sushi with
personality on the side

What to ask for
The history of edomae sushi

Where
1-11-6 Nishi-Azabu,
Minato-ku

When
6 pm—midnight
(closed Sunday)

Robbie Swinnerton

Though no-one can know all of the restaurants in Tokyo, Robbie's knowledge would be hard to match. Born in England, Robbie arrived in Japan in the late 1980s with his wife, Denise, to work in the field of food exporting. The business he worked for was thriving and Robbie was good at his job, but the life of a suit-wearing business traveller wasn't his destiny. He thought about teaching English, as many expats were doing back then (and still are). It was a lucrative job – remember that this was Japan in its boom time. But what Robbie really wanted to do was write.

He managed to get a contract writing a story on China for an English-language newspaper – a seemingly small step, but the first into his new career. Robbie then began work at *The Mainichi*, where he had pitched the idea of a column on food production. From there he became page editor of the travel section. In this role, he commissioned himself (why not?) to start a restaurant page. This was a time when many Japanese chefs were starting to travel and gather influences from other parts of the globe, and overseas chefs were starting to come to Tokyo. It was a time of growth in the quality and quantity of restaurants in Tokyo, particularly those with influences from abroad. Robbie's next role was restaurant critic for *Tokyo Journal* for two years beginning in 1995, and then, two years later, critic for *The Japan Times*, a position he holds to this day.

I have known Robbie for some years now, and have to say he has never steered me wrong in any of his recommendations. Talking to Robbie about the city he calls home – the place that constantly surprises and excites him – always increases my own excitement for the city, tenfold. Robbie has witnessed major shifts in the restaurant scene in Tokyo, and the huge impact that Japanese cuisine has had on the rest of the world, yet he is confident Tokyo's best days are still to come.

GEM by Moto

Who recommended
Robbie Swinnerton

Why
The best sake experience you can have

What to ask for
Leave everything up to Chiba-san

Where
1-30-9 Ebisu, Shibuya-ku

When
5–11.30 pm Tuesday–Friday,
1–9 pm weekends and public holidays

GEM by Moto is one of those places you hear so much about from various sources that by the time you finally get there, you fear the hype might overshadow the actual place.

But with GEM by Moto, this is unlikely. The bright, functional room has a central service area surrounded by bar seating. In the middle of this area, like captain of the ship, stands owner Marie Chiba, overseeing the dockets and pouring the sake. Chiba-san makes you immediately feel welcome. She has an infectious, slightly cheeky smile, and makes eye contact with everyone who enters. As she puts it, she is getting a feel for you, checking your demeanour, sensing your aura, to determine what sake she will serve. Indeed, sake is what this place is all about.

Chiba-san is one of the new breed of sake enthusiasts. She seeks out sakes that are special, perhaps those using older methods of fermentation, or newer strains of yeast, from producers across Japan who are pushing boundaries and giving the drink new life. Chiba-san also has sake made to her own specifications and ages it herself. It follows that you will have a sake experience here like no other. Not only is the sake list unique, but Chiba-san's judicial use of temperature and understanding of texture elevates the experience even further.

Chiba-san will present a sake, ask you to taste it, and then to sprinkle just the smallest amount of sansho pepper on top and try it again. She will serve you a warm sake that she's enhanced with roasted green tea, or maybe a sake finished with a float of beer foam. It's crazy stuff, but it works.

While sake is clearly the focus, the food is no afterthought — because sake is made to be consumed with food. Chiba-san puts as much thought into the food matching as she does into the sake sourcing. Dishes are creative and simple, like sparklingly fresh snapper with just salt and olive oil; a salad of strawberry, melon, tofu, miso and soy; monkfish liver (paired with a lightly sweet genmaishu, or brown-rice sake); a 'sushi' of mackerel and okara, which is the ground soy beans left over from making soy milk; and house-made ramen.

This is a place serious about sake and food, yet it doesn't take itself too seriously. It makes for a fun night out in Tokyo. Like the Willy Wonka of the sake world, Chiba-san is creative and playful, and you can't help but be taken along for the ride.

The clutter and chaos of this
shop made framing up to capture
it an act of intention, and the
authenticity shines through.

Iwashiya

The meaning of the name Iwashiya is 'sardine shop'.

To say Iwashiya specialises in sardines is actually a bit of an understatement. If you don't like sardines, this is not your restaurant. If you do like sardines, it is going to test how much you really like them.

Have the omakase (the chef's set menu) and you will be served up to thirteen courses of sardines prepared in a myriad ways, from sashimi to fried, glazed to grilled. The highlight is without doubt the sardine tsukune: sardines chopped to order, rolled into a ball, wrapped in nori seaweed and poached in a rich dashi stock.

Iwashiya is easy to walk past. I can attest to this – three times over. Nondescript on the outside and a little grungy on the inside, it wears its years with pride. While some might call it shabby, I would say that the place has a wonderful patina created from years of custom and work.

Since Iwashiya is solely centred around one ingredient, the chef is at the mercy of the sardine supply. If supply is low, the restaurant will shut; if it is good, they will open into the early hours of the morning.

This a truly authentic Tokyo experience.

Why
To realise the versatility
of sardines

What to ask for
The tsukune

Where
1-6-5 Hatagaya, Shibuya-ku

When
6.30 pm–4 am weekdays;
6.30 pm–midnight Saturday

The chef is somewhat camera shy; the delicacy of his creations belies the unadorned surrounds.

Kotaro

One element that sets izakayas apart from other restaurants is their emphasis on drinks as much as food.

People come to eat, but also to give the sake selection a good nudge (we're pretty sure it's not just us). Kotaro is the epitome of the modern izakaya – stylish interior, flattering lighting, well-presented chefs, spotless kitchen and a great sake list. Of course it also has creative and delicious food.

Chef and owner Kotaro Hayashi serves dishes from the izakaya canon, but produces them with freshness and lightness, and sometimes a twist, which propels them beyond most others. Dining here had me thinking of one of my first great izakaya experiences in Tokyo, many years ago at a place called KAN, which can still be found in Ikejiri-Ohashi. Then I found out that Kotaro Hayashi was the chef there for many years.

Vegetables play a major role in Kotaro's food and are of excellent quality (Kotaro has personal relationships with his growers, and his seafood is from sustainable sources). There are a number of constants on the menu, such as the classic potato salad where potato is roughly crushed and mixed with other vegetables and mayonnaise. Kotaro's version is finished with a smoked soft-boiled egg and a mustard vinaigrette, taking it above the izakaya standard. Then there is Kotaro's menchi katsu – crumbed and fried patties of minced pork, moist and delicious. A meal here is always finished with handmade udon, served chilled with a simple garnish like grated daikon and soy. This is comfort food, elevated.

Kotaro is very popular, and bookings are difficult to get, so you should plan ahead if you want to secure a table or, even better, a place at the counter. Luke commented that dining here was 'like a hug from your Japanese grandmother', and I agree – though if your grandmother also happens to be a skilled chef with a palate for excellent sake.

Who recommended
Robbie Swinnerton

Why
Izakaya dishes don't get
better than this

What to ask for
Let the chef decide

Where
28-2 Sakuragaokacho,
Shibuya-ku

When
6 pm–1 am (closed Sunday)

Kabi

Why
A glimpse of Tokyo's
next-gen chefs

What to ask for
A seat at the bar

Where
4-10-8 Meguro, Meguro-ku

When
Midday—3 pm weekends,
then from 7 pm (random days;
book in advance)

Kabi is one of the newer and more unique restaurants to open in Tokyo.

It is international in style, with a strong influence from the modern Nordic food movement. Kabi means 'mould' in Japanese, which gives you some indication of what to expect. Fermentation is a big part of both Nordic and Japanese food, and each dish here usually has an element of fermentation, some more funky than others: think miso, natto, black garlic, fermented meats and vegetables.

Kabi is situated in an old building; the facade has been completely remodelled to give the restaurant a modern frontage, but inside are traces of the building's past, particularly the large hand-cut wooden beams and rafters. There are around twenty seats, with thirteen of those at the bar.

The team behind Kabi – Shohei Yasuda, Kentaro Enomoto and Kiriko Nakamura – are young, enthusiastic, confident and earnest.

The dinner menu is set, the wines natural, the sake eclectic. Kabi makes a point of saying that it is not a Japanese restaurant – though there is a focus on Japanese ingredients. The food ranges from exceedingly tasty to more challenging, but the work that goes into each dish is evident, and the plating is beautiful. The menu shows a great deal of creativity but also restraint when it is needed. Tempura sansai (mountain vegetables) is served with just a simple seasoned salt; a clear soup is enhanced with an oil flavoured with binchotan charcoal; raw firefly squid is paired with fermented venison paste and more sansai. This last dish is an example of one that is more cerebral than outright tasty – more about texture and technique – but is fantastic nonetheless. The pickles are stunning, and the desserts made by pastry chef Nakamura are another real highlight. Fukinoto (a vegetable known as the butterbur, with a resinous flavour) makes an appearance in ice-cream with asparagus juice and absinthe – a dessert I still think about.

There is no denying that this is one of Tokyo's 'cool' restaurants, but it has the substance to back it up. I dined there when it was only months old, and it was one of the more intriguing Tokyo meals I've had. I am looking forward to watching Kabi's progression.

Zaiyu Hasegawa

Zaiyu is a joker. His playfulness, his cheeky character, his willingness to toy with tradition are often the first things you read about or notice when dining at his restaurant, Den (2-3-18 Jingumae, Shibuya-ku; 6–11.30 pm, closed Sunday).

Zaiyu and his wife, Emi, have taken the very serious and traditional concept of kaiseki – the multi-course, exquisitely plated haute cuisine of Japan – and imbued with it their own personality. But underneath the humour, seeming relaxation, and even irreverence, is an adherence to technique and to the true meaning of kaiseki. Seasonality is all-important, as is the art of omotenashi, the Japanese concept of hospitality where your needs are anticipated even before you're aware of them. There is a generousness, a true welcome, to the experience at Den.

Zaiyu's food is technical and precise, though this is not necessarily apparent on the plate. What you are presented with are natural, beautiful dishes that taste even better than they look. I have been fortunate to dine at Den at least five times, and each time the bar has been raised.

As with any chef in Tokyo, Zaiyu works long hours, six days a week, so the little amount of free time he has is very important. If Zaiyu chooses to eat at a restaurant, you can be guaranteed he won't be wasting his time on a mediocre one. And this is the reason that getting recommendations from hospitality staff can be so fruitful. They have the connections and know what is happening on the ground, and, being time-poor, they don't stand for average.

Yamamoto

Who recommended
Zaiyu Hasegawa

Why
Brilliant kaiseki worth every yen

What to ask for
Just sit back and let it happen

Where
46-10 Oyamacho, Shibuya-ku

When
From 7 pm
Wednesday—Monday

In Tokyo, word of mouth is very important, especially for a restaurant as tucked away as Yamamoto.

When that word of mouth comes from one of Tokyo's most respected and well-known chefs, you pay attention. Zaiyu Hasegawa (see page 174) listed this as his favourite Japanese restaurant in Tokyo. To say we had high expectations was an understatement.

Yamamoto opened in 2013 but has been in its current location since 2016: the basement of the nondescript J's Building near Yoyogi-Uehara station. With real estate at such a premium in Tokyo, factors such as location, street frontage and views are less of a consideration. There are eight seats at a bar overlooking an open kitchen and another six seats in a private dining room. The bar is made of hinoki (Japanese cypress), and it is where you want to be for watching Yamamoto-san at work. It should keep you entranced over the next few hours.

While you can spend a whole lot more on kaiseki in Tokyo, most people would consider that the cost of the meal at Yamamoto still makes it a big-ticket event. Yamamoto-san trained as a sushi chef before moving into kaiseki here. Kaiseki is Japan's revered cuisine featuring many courses, artful presentation and ultra seasonality. As you'd expect, the sushi component of Yamamoto-san's food is superb.

Our meal started with an exquisite bowl of raw seafood with different temperatures and textures – crunchy herring roe, warm sea urchin, creamy tuna with miso, and chewy smoked razor clam – then progressed through ten generous courses in a classic kaiseki format. Fried lotus, shiitake, fugu (the famous blowfish with some poisonous body parts) paired with gingko, dobin mushi (teapot soup) with intensely flavoured matsutake mushrooms, amazing nodoguro (black-throat sea perch) smoked over rice straw. The final rice course, a given in kaiseki, involves rice cooked in a hotpot; on this occasion ours was topped with unpasteurised salmon roe and baby sardines cooked in sweetened soy sauce.

Yamamoto-san and his mother are the only staff of the restaurant. Throughout our meal, they went to great lengths to explain the food in English as best they could, using a collection of books, Google and their actually very capable language skills. They truly want you to know the intricacies of your meal, and their enthusiasm is a joy.

The line and form of the 300-year-old
hinoki counter screamed black
   and white, allowing the texture of the
wood to shine through.

Fuku and Le Cabaret

If there is one genre of food in Japan that exists at all levels, it is yakitori.

You will find it in casual lunch venues, in refined dinner restaurants, and in dingy, late-night diners where your choice of seating could well be a sake crate. It is also often part of the repertoire of izakaya chefs. But one thing all yakitori venues have in common is a sense of revelry: the rooms are always a bit louder; the drinks flow faster. Barbecues are the sort of cooking that encourages conversation, and yakitori is no exception.

Fuku is at the more sophisticated end of the yakitori spectrum; however, the extensive selection of chicken and vegetable skewers is fairly reasonably priced. The room is modern and spacious, but, as always in Tokyo, nab a spot at the counter if possible.

Fuku is certainly one of the most welcoming Tokyo restaurants I have been to. The crowd is younger than most yakitori venues, and there is usually a smattering of gaijin, or foreigners, in the restaurant – the friendly staff are very accommodating to non-Japanese speakers.

It is ideal to book, but you can attempt to walk in either earlier or later in the evening. The restaurant manager is very helpful and will try his hardest to fit you in. There may still be a wait, but this is a good thing, because then you can spend your waiting time at Le Cabaret, a fantastic wine bar just two minutes walk away.

Le Cabaret is one of the more popular natural wine bars in Tokyo, like Ahiru Store (see page 139), and was also one of the first. If you're wanting something different for dinner, Le Cabaret is also a food destination in its own right, offering simple, classic French fare to match their wine list.

pét nat
Vin Blanc
Rosé
Rouge   10⁰⁰ ~
Bière Blanche   9⁵⁰
SAPPORO   6⁰⁰
        etc.
Pastis 51   6⁰⁰
Monkey 47 Tonic 12⁰⁰

" Eau de Vie "
Framboise
Marc
Calvados
Armagnac
Rhum JM XO 12⁰⁰ ~

Chateldon 75cl   12⁰⁰

Café   4⁰⁰
Café allongé   5⁰⁰
Noisette   ~
Café crème   6⁰⁰
Infusions   6⁵⁰

youpi les Brebis!

Fuku

Why

Excellent yakitori in a
vibrant setting

What to ask for

A place at the counter to watch
the action, of course

Where

3-23-4 Nishihara, Shibuya-ku

When

5.30–11.30 pm
(closed Wednesday)

Le Cabaret

Why

The best waiting bar you
could ask for

What to ask for

The oysters (always so fresh)

Where

8-8 Motoyoyogicho,
Shibuya-ku

When

6 pm–midnight (closed Monday
and occasionally Tuesday)

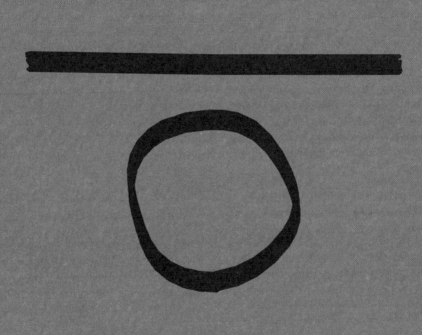

189

Bar Benfiddich

You've walked down a backstreet and somehow found your destination, entered the multistorey building, travelled up to the required floor.

When you pass the threshold of the mundane, utilitarian entrance, you're in another world. This happens so often in Tokyo. Magical and unique spaces have been created in the most unlikely of locations.

In the case of Bar Benfiddich, the space is a kind of cross between the inside of a pirate ship, an apothecary, and a bar from the set of a fantasy movie. And the man behind the bar, Hiroyasu Kayama, looks just as fabulous. Dressed impeccably in a white dinner coat with a pocket square and matching tie, tiepin, wingtip collar and cufflinks, he manages to still look sharp at the end of the night.

His attention to detail also applies to the cocktails. As with many of Japan's cocktail bars, there is no menu here, and you are asked what sort of cocktail you might be after. Sure Kayama-san can do the classics (though his bar leans towards whisky and rye, gin and absinthe), but you really should let him create something for you from the collection of infusions and tinctures he has lined up at the back of the bar.

He is famous for his 'Campari' that he makes using a large mortar and pestle, a little vodka and eleven different herbs and spices, including cochineal, the colour derived from small insects that gave Campari its red hue up until a decade ago. Bar Benfiddich's version of the drink is quite different – more bitter and herbal, certainly more interesting.

Another good option is to ask for an amaro-based cocktail. Kayama-san has an obsession with amaro, that category of similarly bitter, herbal liqueurs of Italian origin. (Campari is not always considered a member of the family, partly because it is usually served before rather than after a meal.) Of course Kayama-san makes his own amaro on the spot. The most recent one I had featured gin and fresh wormwood ground in a large antique Chinese tea grinder, garnished with lemon and honey.

Kayama-san makes every cocktail, but like the magic show that this is, he has two assistants either side seamlessly supplying him with the tools he needs. This bar is most definitely in the 'only in Tokyo' category.

Why
'Campari' like no other

What to ask for
Let Kayama-san work his magic

Where
9th floor, 1-13-7 Nishi-Shinjuku,
Shinjuku-ku

When
6 pm–3 am (closed Sunday)

Melinda
Joe

Melinda came to Tokyo from Louisiana fourteen years ago, with no intention to stay too long. But the place got under her skin, and then she met her husband, JP, who was working at a university. She'd always had a strong interest in all things food and drink, and so as a side interest she started writing a blog. This was right at that time when blogs were big, and when the world's fascination with Japan was starting to explode, and Melinda's inside knowledge became sought after. She now writes for many publications including *Newsweek*, *The Wall Street Journal*, Swedish magazine *Gourmet*, and the *South China Morning Post*. Much of her writing is about restaurants and food, but she also has a keen interest in and great knowledge of sake.

Melinda has lived in Tokyo during a time of great growth in the restaurant scene. While younger chefs have been pushing more and more boundaries, the interest in traditional Japanese cuisine has been growing as well. She has witnessed the exponential growth in tourists coming to Tokyo because of its restaurants, and is there now to see the inevitable backlash. A few high-end restaurants are refusing to take bookings from non-Japanese people unless the bookings come through a hotel, and in some cases not at all. The reasons for this are complex, but late cancellations, no-shows and ignorance of accepted behaviours are big components. Most of these restaurants are quite small, so they can afford to be selective. However, remember that in Tokyo, there is always another restaurant.

Melinda loves that no matter how much you think you know about Tokyo, there is always more to explore, another layer to discover inside the city's seemingly disorganised vastness and pace. Some of my most memorable nights in the city have been with Melinda and JP. In fact, in an admission that would be shocking to some, Melinda is the only person who has ever dragged me out to karaoke in my many trips to the city.

Yata

Who recommended
Melinda Joe

Why
An inexpensive but
sophisticated tachinomiya

What to ask for
The all-you-can-drink-
in-one-hour deal

Where
10th floor, 3-14-22 Shinjuku,
Shinjuku-ku, and 1-6-1
Dogenzaka, Shibuya-ku

When
5—11.30 pm Tuesday—Friday,
1—9 pm weekends and
public holidays

Tachinomiya — standing bars — are a distinctly Japanese concept.

When space is at a premium, the idea of bars (and some restaurants) offering only standing room makes perfect sense. With no seating to worry about, you can fit a whole lot more customers in. Most tachinomiya are cheap and cheerful, without frills.

Yata in Shinjuku (they have a branch in Shibuya as well) is a little different, with the decor and lighting of a sophisticated bar. It is located on the tenth floor of a building in a busy part of town. The building is hard to find, but we knew we were in the right place when a very drunk Japanese man fell out of the elevator, let out a scream of delight on seeing three gaijin (foreigners), and directed us to the correct floor.

Yata's focus is on sake, and we soon worked out why the fellow in the lift was so inebriated: as well as an 'à la carte' option, where you can choose glasses of sake for around 500 yen each, there is an all-you-can-drink-in-one-hour option at 2000 yen — economical but dangerous.

Given this, you might think the sake wouldn't be of the highest standard, but their selection — all junmai, or pure rice wine without distilled alcohol added — is quite extensive and good quality, and changes regularly. The range may be a little more mainstream than that of, say, GEM by Moto (see page 158), but the staff here are truly passionate about the drink and happy to guide you through the choices. Snacks are available, but really, you come for the sake.

Wine Stand Waltz

**Going to Waltz feels like being invited
over to your cool uncle's house.**

The owner – and sole staff member – Yasuhiro Ooyama, is a wonderfully generous and gregarious host, and his enthusiasm for wine is obvious. The wines available are all from his personal collection. The selection has a strong bent towards wines of the Jura, particularly of the natural persuasion, along with wines from Japanese winemakers, both within Japan and overseas.

Waltz is another tachinomi or standing bar (tachi means 'stand' and nomi means 'drink'), with space for maybe just eight people. The tiny room is decorated with French art and film paraphernalia.

Ooyama whips up a few light snacks through the evening, adding to the feeling that you really could just be in his lounge room.

Waltz makes for a perfect pre- or post-dinner destination.

Why
To rub shoulders, literally, with Tokyo's wine buffs

What to ask for
A bit of luck to get a space

Where
4-24-3 Ebisu, Shibuya-ku

When
6 pm–midnight (closed Sunday)

Bar Orchard Ginza

Tokyo is not short on cocktail bars: casual, serious, private, public, modern, classic. But none are quite like Bar Orchard Ginza.

No menu is offered, but your attention is directed to a large display of fruit and vegetables in the centre of the bar (the bar's name now makes sense). Pick your fruit or vegetable, and the staff will ask you a few questions, learning of your likes and dislikes, determining what style of cocktails you are into – strong or weak, more sweet or sour, long or short. Then they'll set about making a cocktail just for you.

With the cocktails based on fruits and vegetables, they tend to be lighter and fresher, and certainly less spirit-forward than many of the classics. Modern techniques are used, including liquid nitrogen and smoking guns, and the presentation is, well, unique. One cocktail might be in a small plastic bathtub complete with floating yellow ducks; another might be in a replica wheelie bin; yet another is presented in a toy coffin, dry-ice fumes flowing from the casket. This is a cocktail bar where kawaii culture is king.

Anywhere else, this might come across as gimmicky or cheesy, but the enthusiasm of the owners – husband and wife Sumire and Takuo Miyanohara – is infectious. Dressed in matching denim overalls, they seem a cross between old-school confectioners and magicians. They speak excellent English and go out of their way to make sure every guest has a great time. I can't think of a cocktail bar in Tokyo that is more fun.

Who recommended
Makiko Iitsuka
and Kenichi Yamamoto

Why
Personalised cocktails without
pretension

What to ask for
Your favourite fruit

Where
7th floor, 6-5-16 Ginza, Chuo-ku

When
6 pm–1 am (closed Sunday)

Makiko Iitsuka &
Kenichi Yamamoto

Makiko and Kenichi's restaurant, Les Alchimistes (1-25-26 Shirokane, Minato-ku; midday–3 pm Friday–Tuesday, 6–11.30 pm Thursday–Tuesday), is the epitome of a small partner-run restaurant in Tokyo. The two of them work seamlessly together, each extremely talented in their own field. With just fourteen seats, dining at Les Alchimistes feels like you've been invited into the home of friends. That is, if those friends happen to be a brilliant chef and an extremely talented sommelier.

Kenichi runs the kitchen, producing artful plates of delicious food from a tiny, immaculate kitchen. There is a lot of technique to his food, but on the plate it has an elegant simplicity. Kenichi's food reflects – as all good food should – his life experiences, work history, interests. Originally from Osaka, Kenichi has also worked at the highly regarded Le Chateaubriand in Paris.

Makiko runs the front of house, and does it with the confidence of someone who knows everything the job entails. She came to hospitality on a more circuitous route. Born in Ibaraki prefecture north-east of Tokyo, she too lived in Paris for some time. She moved there to study ballet, and it was in Paris that Kenichi and Makiko met. She is one of the more charming restaurant hosts I have met in Tokyo. As with so many other new-generation sommeliers in the city, she has a great interest and passion for lo-fi, organic and biodynamic wines.

Kenichi and Makiko love what Tokyo offers in terms of restaurants, bars and people, and can't think of anywhere else they would rather be.

Kouei

We've all been to late-night restaurants like Kouei, with people hungry from too much booze and hospo staff chilling after hard services.

Then again, you may not have been to a place exactly like Kouei. This is a yakiniku restaurant, which is what happens when the Japanese turn to Korean barbecue. This yakiniku specialises in offal – horumon in Japanese. Some say this word is derived from the English 'hormone', which is how you often see it translated on menus. It may also come from the words 'horu mono' from a Japanese dialect, meaning 'that which is thrown away'. Horumon can include liver, intestine, lung, heart, uterus – the Japanese know all about nose-to-tail eating.

The meat is often marinated in a spicy sauce, which smokes and chars on the charcoal brazier in the middle of the table. When dining with a group, it is usually best to nominate a chef (you know, too many cooks …). We were fortunate enough to have Zaiyu Hasegawa, one of Tokyo's finest chefs (see page 174), on the job. Accompaniments to the grilled meats include kimchi (the Japanese style is different to Korean – sweeter, with less heat); yukke, a raw beef dish similar to tartare; vegetables, equally great on the grill as the meat; and usually a salad.

Excuse the pun, but this is gutsy food, perfect to soak up those one or two drinks too many. Service is straight to the point with the food arriving promptly, and the beers even quicker.

Who recommended
Zaiyu Hasegawa

Why
You can't go all night without
sustenance

What to ask for
The offal

Where
2-4-11 Kabukicho, Shinjuku-ku

When
5 pm–4 am daily

Bunon

There are many wine bars in Tokyo focusing on natural, low-interventionist wine, nearly all modelled on the wine bars of Europe.

The food on offer is the classic wine pairings: charcuterie, cheeses, steaks, et al. The decor usually borrows from Europe as well, with darkly wooded interiors, bentwood furniture and candlelight. Bunon caters to all your lo-fi wine needs with one of the better lists in the city – but it differs in decor and food. Located between two unremarkable buildings, the entrance looks like something out of a Japanese fairytale. Enter through that door and you are in a restored old Japanese house with straw and mud walls and shoji screens. The food matches the traditional vibe: think sashimi, excellent fried kuwai (a little potato-like vegetable that if you ever see on a menu, you must order), fried shirako (cod sperm sacs – if you visit Japan in winter, you'll probably come across this ingredient), and delicious vegetable dishes. The Japanese menu can be tricky, but if you just let the chefs send out some stuff, you can't really go wrong.

The other thing that makes Bunon so enjoyable is the staff. Show some interest and enthusiasm in the wine and you will get it back threefold. Chef and owner Shigeru Nakaminato is a wonderfully gregarious fellow with seemingly endless energy. The place is open late and Nakaminato-san never seems to stop. But just one word of warning: Nakaminato-san is in demand at many food and wine events overseas, so Bunon closes when he is attending these.

Why
Natural wines are rarely paired
with great Japanese food

What to ask for
Any of the seasonal dishes on offer

Where
4-2-14 Nishi-Azabu, Minato-ku

When
6 pm–midnight Monday–Wednesday,
6 pm–2 am Thursday–Saturday

Grandfather's

Why
A relaxed end to your night

What to ask for
Your favourite track

Where
1-24-7 Shibuya, Shibuya-ku

When
5 pm–3 am daily

The diffusion of light through
smoke in this dimly lit basement
made for a few hours of bliss.

There is a kind of bar in Japan, and in particular in Tokyo, that you just don't see anywhere else in the world: the vinyl bar.

Always small, often smoky and usually hard to find, these bars have a large selection of vinyl albums that are played throughout the night by a DJ behind the bar. The DJs are invariably hi-fi obsessives, and some of the equipment I have seen in these small bars would easily be worth hundreds of thousands of dollars — Tannoy speakers and McIntosh amps are common. Each bar tends to specialise in a genre, with jazz being one of the more popular.

Some vinyl bars can be very serious. Loud talking is often frowned upon; you are there to enjoy the music and the sound, and will be asked to leave if you are too noisy. Grandfather's has a much more relaxed vibe, though it is still not a place for a rowdy evening.

The music at Grandfather's encompasses rock from the 1950s and '60s and soul and funk from the '70s, with a smattering of '60s and '70s folk. The room has a smokiness to match the vintage tunes, so be prepared for that, but the throwback drink prices are very reasonable. Anyway, your sole focus soon becomes the music — what the current track is, what the next track will be, and how good vinyl can sound.

You are free to request a song; just keep their genre in mind. Write your request on a piece of paper and hand it to the waiter, who will pass it to the DJ. If they have the song, they will play it, though perhaps not immediately. It is a perfect business model, as it keeps you there, drinking, waiting for your song to come on. Then as soon as your song is played you want to request another, and so it goes until you realise you have been there all night and have probably drunk just a bit too much. But it is so much fun, you will want to do it all again the next night.

Bar Trench

There is no denying that the cocktail scene in Tokyo has had a huge impact around the world.

Places like Tender, Bar High Five and Star Bar, all in Ginza, were perfecting and preserving the art of the classic cocktail while the West was going through the 'bad years' of the 1970s and '80s, when nearly every cocktail had either cream or milk in it. With the passing of time and changes in trends, the West rediscovered classic cocktails, and also discovered that some of the best versions were being made in Tokyo.

Yet while Japan led the way, some of its bars were so strict and prescriptive that the creative side of cocktail making and bartending was missing. It could be said that over-creative bartending sent cocktails to a new dark side, but there is a middle ground.

Bar Trench straddles that difficult border between tradition and creativity with perfection. Opened in 2010, it is one of my favourite places in Tokyo. The interior is dark and moody, with crystal light-fittings and glassware, and a mezzanine set up as a library, giving the place the look of an old-world Paris bar. The emphasis on absinthe heightens that feeling. But absinthe is not a total obsession, as the drinks here have great diversity. Cocktails range from straight-up classics, to modern interpretations, to unique one-off creations.

The playlist here is the final small detail that makes this place so enjoyable: eclectic and perfectly in tune with the mood of the bar.

Bar Trench is small, with space for maybe fifteen. If you don't have any luck getting in, the group behind the bar have two others nearby — Bar Tram and Bar Triad. Between the three of them, you won't go thirsty.

Why
Perfectly crafted cocktails in
an atmospheric setting

What to ask for
Something with absinthe to start

Where
1-5-8 Ebisu-Nishi, Shibuya-ku

When
7 pm–2 am Monday–Saturday,
6 pm–1 am Sunday and public holidays

Getting Around Tokyo

On the macro scale (getting from one station to another, or one area to another), it is surprisingly easy getting around Tokyo. The Tokyo Metro subway system is well organised, efficient and always on time. The JR and private lines, equally so. A Suica or Pasmo card (pre-paid travel cards available from ticket machines at most large stations) is a great investment, and these cards can be used on all train lines and even in vending machines and taxis. The bus system in Tokyo is also very good, but does require another layer of knowledge and navigational skills (because you need to figure out which stops to get on and off at).

The difficulty with buses is partly because, on the micro level in Japan – in streets and blocks – things can get a little unstuck. Finding your destination on foot is equally tricky. Usually only the more major streets have names, e.g. Aoyama-dori, Takeshita-dori (fashion hub of Harajuku). A lot of the street names are colloquial, e.g. Cat Street.

The Japanese address system works like a funnel going from a large to small geographical scale. In place of street names is a series of usually three numbers, where the first number designates the neighbourhood, the next the block, then the building. However, the buildings on any given block are numbered based on when they were registered, meaning that the numbers don't run in any linear order. Even locals have trouble finding their way, and taxi drivers aren't much better. Google Maps can be a real friend. Another handy trick is to do an image search on Google, of both the front of the building and its Japanese sign – then when you're locating the building, you don't need to be able to read Kanji, but just have the ability to find the match. Always allow extra time before a restaurant booking to locate an unfamiliar place.

Index by Category

Authors

Michael Ryan is one of Australia's most respected chefs. With partner Jeanette Henderson, he is the owner of Provenance Restaurant in Beechworth, north-east Victoria.

After initially studying science at the University of Adelaide and working in chemistry for several years, Michael opened his first restaurant with Jeanette, Range, in 2006. Range won a succession of two-hat awards in *The Age Good Food Guide*, as well as Country Restaurant of the Year in 2008. Provenance opened in early 2009 and has since gone on to receive two hats every year since. In 2013, Provenance won Best Regional Restaurant and Michael Ryan was named Chef of the Year.

Michael has a long-term interest in Japanese cuisine, and this is reflected in the techniques and flavours used in the Provenance menus. He also hosts small-group guided tours to Japan each year.

Luke Burgess finished his apprenticeship at renowned Sydney restaurant Tetsuya's before embarking on a career in freelance food and travel photography.

In 2006 Luke and his partner moved to Tasmania in search of a culinary adventure and soon after opened Pecora Café. A couple of years later, inspired by a stint at Copenhagen's Noma, Luke and business partners Katrina Birchmeier and Kirk Richardson opened Garagistes in Hobart. In 2011, Luke won Best New Talent in the Gourmet Traveller Restaurant Awards, and Garagistes scored two stars in the *Gourmet Traveller Restaurant Guide* and was listed in Australia's top 100 restaurants.

Since closing Garagistes in 2015, Luke has cooked in eight different countries, run Sydney's 10 William St for five months, and started a company consulting to emerging hospitality ventures.

Acknowledgements

My first thank you is to Karyn Noble, now senior editor at Lonely Planet in London. She stayed and dined with us some years back and was so encouraging of my naive interest in writing a book. It was her introduction to Jane Willson at Hardie Grant that led to this book.

Jane was kind enough to listen to my first ideas for what initially was a very different project, and gave us both freedom and direction when needed. Thanks also to Emily Hart and Vanessa Masci from Hardie Grant for their expertise and ideas, and to my editor, Rachel Pitts, for being so thorough and making me look like a better writer than I am.

Extra special thanks to my wife and business partner, Jeanette Henderson. She has always been my muse and my most honest critic, and her input is hidden all through this book.

Finally, thank you to Luke Burgess, whose images perfectly matched my concept of what this book was going to be and who helped shape it into what it became.

— Michael

An idea discussed over a post-service beer on the River Torrens with Michael Ryan set this book in motion. It wouldn't have been possible without Michael's wit, humour and deep love of Japan, which opened many a door. Both you and Jeanette made our travels unforgettable.

I would also like to thank Jane Willson for courting the idea and rolling the dice. Your energy and passion for our project was essential. The team at Hardie Grant, your ability to understand exactly what we wanted this book to look and feel like was an immense source of satisfaction.

To all the photographers who allowed me to escape the kitchen and indulge my other passion, and whose mentorship and work shaped the way I see the world, I cannot thank you enough.

Finally, the complete Tokyo crew who welcomed me on my numerous trips, your kindness and genuine hospitality was world class. To Ayaka, Masa, Miku and Shin, the deep sense of pride in your city, its people and its labyrinth of places made for a truly unique insight into Japanese culture.

— Luke

Published in 2019 by Hardie Grant Books,
an imprint of Hardie Grant Publishing

Hardie Grant Books (Melbourne)
Building 1, 658 Church Street
Richmond, Victoria 3121

Hardie Grant Books (London)
5th & 6th Floors
52–54 Southwark Street
London SE1 1UN

hardiegrantbooks.com

 A catalogue record for this
book is available from the
National Library of Australia

Only in Tokyo
ISBN 978 1 74379 479 1

10 9 8 7 6 5 4 3 2 1

Publishing Director: Jane Willson
Project Editor: Emily Hart
Editor: Rachel Pitts
Design Manager: Jessica Lowe
Designer: Vanessa Masci
Production Manager: Todd Rechner

Colour reproduction by Splitting Image Colour Studio
Printed in China by Leo Paper Product. LTD